Becoming a Disciple of Truth

A guide on how to become and to help others become intentional, committed and effective Disciples of Christ

Mike Miles

"**Becoming a Disciple of Truth** is not everything you should know about Christianity, but it's a good place to start."

When you read this book, you will be challenged to become more committed and intentional in pursuing God and helping others do the same.

__Becoming a Disciple of Truth__ is a helpful resource enabling the reader to quickly receive a general overall understanding of Christianity. It contains bible history, current events, scriptures, questions, answers and "tools" to stimulate the growth of the curious and the believer.

__Becoming a Disciple of Truth__ is an ideal first step in leading people toward the Bible and a vibrant living relationship with the Lord. It also presents a challenge to current believers to seek a deeper walk with God.

__Becoming a Disciple of Truth__ is user-friendly and an excellent tool for assisting in personal evangelism, mentoring, bible studies and discipleship training.

© 2017 ISBN: 978-1978024205

For copies, comments or to support the distribution of this book, contact Brushfire Publications at:
P. O. Box 777 – Youngsville, LA 70592
Phone: 337-781-3280
e-mail: mcmilesjr@yahoo.com

Dedication

"This book is dedicated to all those who have gone before, and all those who now and in the future, will commit themselves to making the greatest difference possible for the cause of Christ."

Scripture Bible References Used in
<u>Becoming a Disciple of Truth</u>

(NKJV) – New King James Version
(NLT) – New Living Translation

These two translations of the Bible used for reference in <u>Becoming a Disciple of Truth,</u> gives today's reader a good overall understanding of the Bible's intended meaning, without the challenging formality associated with the Old English found in the pure King James Version or the slight misrepresentations or omissions found in a few of the other modern day Bible translations.

TABLE OF CONTENTS

OUTLINE FOR DISCIPLESHIP & BIBLE STUDY CLASSES	p. 6
INTRODUCTION	p. 15
CHAPTER 1 - THE WAR BEGINS	p. 19
CHAPTER 2 - PRIDE, THE STUMBLING BLOCK	p. 23
CHAPTER 3 - MAN STRUGGLES/GOD RESTORES	p. 27
CHAPTER 4 - CHRISTIANITY vs. OTHER RELIGIONS	p. 33
CHAPTER 5 - A FLAWED ATHEIST PERSPECTIVE	p. 37
CHAPTER 6 - THINK YOU MIGHT BE A CHRISTIAN?	p. 43
CHAPTER 7 - CHRISTIANS & "LOOK-A-LIKES"	p. 49
CHAPTER 8 - HEAVEN IS OPTIONAL	p. 55
CHAPTER 9 - ADVERSITY'S SILVER LINING	p. 61
CHAPTER 10 – TRINITY DISCILPSHIP	p. 65
CHAPTER 11 - YOUR STORY/HIS GLORY	p. 73
CHAPTER 12 - AMBASSADORS OF GOD'S LOVE	p. 77
CHAPTER 13 - ESCAPING "LUKEWARM	p. 87
CHAPTER 14 - KNOWING THE LORD	p. 95
CHAPTER 15 - GOD'S BLUEPRINT –THE BIBLE	p. 103
CHAPTER 16 - TIMES AND MISSION OF JESUS	p. 111
CHAPTER 17 - IN ONE ACCORD?	p. 117
CHAPTER 18 - THE PERSON OF THE HOLY SPIRIT	p. 123
CHAPTER 19 - DON'T STOP HIM	p. 133

TABLE OF CONTENTS

CHAPTER 20 - SIGNS OF THE TIMES	p. 139
CHAPTER 21 - THE DECEPTION OF COMPROMISE	p. 147
CHAPTER 22 - ENEMY STRONGHOLDS	p. 153
CHAPTER 23 - CHRISTIAN WEAPONS OF WAR	p. 161
CHAPTER 24 - ONCE SAVED, ALWAYS SAVED?	p. 171
CHAPTER 25 - A TALE OF TWO NATIONS	p. 179
CHAPTER 26 - GOD'S PEOPLE PERSECUTED	p. 187
CHAPTER 27 - THE COUNTERFEIT GOD	p. 193
CHAPTER 28 - RAPTURE & THE SECOND COMING	p. 203
CHAPTER 29 - THE GREAT WHITE HARVEST	p. 209
CHAPTER 30 - THE LIST	p. 214
CHAPTER 31- THE VALLEY OF DECISION	p. 218
CHAPTER 32 - THE LAST CHAPTER	p. 222
KEYS TO AN EFFECTIVE CHRISTIAN LIFESTYLE	p. 230
YOU ARE WHO HE SAYS YOU ARE	p. 235
A DISCIPLES CHECKLIST	p. 236
THREE PRAYER TEMPLETS	p. 239
HELPFUL SCRIPTURES	p. 248
LIST OF RECOMMENDED BOOKS	p. 266
TOPIC LOCATOR FOR THIS BOOK	p. 268

OUTLINE FOR DISCIPLESHIP & BIBLE STUDY CLASSES

1. It is suggested that the following format be used for weekly assignments and homework review.

WEEK 1	ORIENTATION / PREVIEW PGS. 5 -18
WEEK 2	READ AND REVIEW CHAPTERS 1-5
WEEK 3	READ AND REVIEW CHAPTERS 6-10
WEEK 4	READ AND REVIEW CHAPTERS 11-14
WEEK 5	READ AND REVIEW CHAPTERS 15-19
WEEK 6	READ AND REVIEW CHAPTERS 20-24
WEEK 7	READ AND REVIEW CHAPTERS 25-29
WEEK 8	READ AND REVIEW CHAPTERS 30-32

2. In the Week 1 session, participants introduce themselves, receive a copy of this book and are guided through pages 5-18. Whether used for classes or individual discipleship, the "identity" of a disciple of Christ should be discussed, using the "You Are Who He Says You Are" list on page 236 in the back of the book. Sessions should last approximately one hour. **Each week, participants briefly share what God has done in their lives followed by reviewing the questions for the week's assigned chapters.**

3. At the end of each session, assign the next group of chapters and questions for daily study. Resources and assignments beyond those contained in this book can be included as each group leader deems appropriate. Be sure to include ministry time to encourage participants and for those requesting prayer for specific needs.

Why Write "Becoming a Disciple of Truth"?

Over the years I realized I wanted to have a resource to leave with people that would expand their overall understanding of Jesus' victory, the ministry of the Holy Spirit, Bible history and the responsibility of Christians in today's turbulent times. I was inspired by my doctor Baljinder Kumar, my teenage daughter Paula and her "millennial" generation, to create a user-friendly introduction to Christianity.

In over 30 plus years as a lay minister I've served as a church videographer, deacon, led people in the "sinner's prayer" in numerous public and private settings, taught classes, assisted with plays, have been a small group leader and early on went into Louisiana prisons with Inner-Faith Prison Ministry.

Pastor R. S. King was my first spiritual mentor and greatly impacted my life. We currently attend the Vineyard Church of Lafayette, Louisiana where Pastors Dino and Kris Griffin, as well as other area pastors, have shared our desire to better understand humanity, the believer's responsibility for discipleship, and also heightened our appreciation for the majesty of Christ's divinity. I've seen many lives dramatically transformed by the power of God's love. It's my hope this book blesses and encourages you, and is a tool that helps you as you impact others for the cause of Christ.

Acknowledgments

The circle of friends and family that God has placed in my life are largely responsible for this book coming into existence. Paul Atkins, the "brother I never had" has been a faithful and true friend since the day we met over 40 years ago. Anthony C. Rock, Margaret and Allen Beyer, Rick and Lynn Oglesbee, Paul Tharp, Nate Moore, Scott Malagarie, Brian Beduze, Linda Moody and Ann Alexander have been supportive, consistent and positive influences in helping to bring <u>Becoming a Disciple of Truth</u> to others.

A very special thanks goes to my wife Jerelyn, as she so faithfully partnered with me throughout this entire project. Pastors Richard Ledet and Kenneth Leleux provided wise counsel, helping to maintain Biblical accuracy. Brenda Tharp carefully helped with the initial "fine tuning" and Gil Broussard added his crucial technical expertise. Thank you!!!

It is our hope that this book, by the power of the Holy Spirit, will bring the unbeliever to faith in Christ and compel current believers to fully embrace God's calling on their life and ministry.

There are other *"Pauls"* and many *"rock solid"* influences in my life that are too numerous to mention here. There is someone however, who more than any other deserves all the praise, all the glory and all the honor for this book. Hopefully, you will find Him in the following pages.

In one of the last sermons Pastor R.S. King preached he said, *"If you remember nothing else about this message, remember this, **it's all about others.**"* He also said that it was his hope that some of the good things he did would live on after him. He then challenged those in attendance to impact the lives of others.

"Let nothing be done through selfish ambition or conceit, but in lowliness of mind let each esteem others better than himself. Let each of you look out not only for his own interests, but also for the interests of others. Let this mind be in you which was also in Christ Jesus." Philippians 2:3-5 (NKJV)

This book as well as many other efforts Pastor King supported, are in part the fulfillment of his hope.

~~~~~~~

<u>Becoming a Disciple of Truth</u> is a no-frills rocket ride through centuries of recorded history. This informative, historical overview is designed to give all readers a broad understanding of God's plan to reconcile not only man's realm, but also to bring judgment to Satan and his demonic angel followers in the spiritual realm.

This two-fold process is being accomplished in and through the obedience and ultimate victory of Jesus Christ, the one and only Son of God.

Author's Note

<u>Becoming a Disciple of Truth</u> has the potential to awaken the spiritually stagnant, to help convict the sinner of the need to accept Jesus Christ as Savior, and even to encourage those who are spiritually hungry to be more intentional in their pursuit of what God has for them.

It has been a "work in progress" and used in discipleship classes and bible studies. There have been many obstacles to getting it to the point where it can begin to impact others.

If you read one of the earliest versions of this book, you may notice some typos and or grammatical errors. Also, throughout the book there are some thoughts and scriptures repeated because quite often, we need to hear or read something several times before it really sinks in.

In the near future, our plan is to build a website where <u>Becoming a Disciple of Truth</u> will be available as a PDF download.

Any delay in getting this into the hands of those who could benefit from it is troubling, especially given all the warning signs that are escalating throughout the world today. Therefore, I humbly ask you to forgive my literary limitations and enjoy the effort of one disciple of truth, to inspire and equip other disciples of truth.

The "Spear into the Darkness Project"

The most effective weapon against the evil deceit and darkness of the world is the light of God's truth. We call the launching of this book, the "Spear into the Darkness Project". It is just one of many ways God is reaching the world with the light of His truth.

We realize that those who oppose the one true and living God will attempt to block the influence of this book at every opportunity. Nevertheless, at God's leading and with the help of others, this book will influence many.

Christian ministries who share our belief in the responsibility and opportunity the Great Commission affords us are encouraged to consider including <u>Becoming a Disciple of Truth</u> as a part of their ministry resource offering. Every effort will be made to assist partnering groups to acquire the book at bulk discounted rates and drop-shipped directly to their designated locations.

Amongst the many worthwhile ministry efforts to consider, <u>Becoming a Disciple of Truth</u> may be a project that the Lord will direct you to support. If so, please make your orders and/or donations toward the cost and distribution of the books to:

Brushfire Publications
P. O. Box 777 - Youngsville, LA 70592

A BRIEF CHRONOLOGY OF SOME KEY BIBLE EVENTS

1. Satan, the devil and 1/3 of the angels in heaven are cast out of heaven as a result of the rebellion started by Satan. (Rev. 12:4 - Rev. 12:9)
2. God creates man (Adam and Eve) in His own image. (Genesis 1:27)
3. Satan deceives Eve. Adam and Eve disobey God and as a result their God-given nature was changed and infected with sin and rebellion. (Genesis 3: 1-7)
4. God destroys most of mankind with a great flood, but spares a righteous man called Noah and his family with whom he begins to re-populate the earth. (Genesis chapters 6-8)
5. God makes a covenant with Abraham that requires faith and obedience. (Gen 17:1-8)
6. The Old Testament of the Bible describes how God's chosen people (called the Jews, Hebrews or Israelites) did or did not serve and obey God as they interacted with the rest of mankind. The **Old Testament** also prophesied the coming of one descendent of Abraham - Jesus, God's Son. He was sent from heaven to be born as a man, live a sinless life and

sacrifice His life to pay for mankind's rebellion and sin. (John 3:16-18))
7. The first four books of the **New Testament** proclaim the Good News of Jesus' life, death, resurrection from the dead and ascension into heaven (**the Gospels**).
8. In other New Testament books (Acts through Jude), the Holy Spirit of God teaches mankind how to live for God. Jesus' early followers and His disciples along with the Apostle Paul, wrote the New Testament. It describes the activities of the early believers in Jesus and the development of His church.
9. In both the Old Testament and the New Testament there is considerable prophecy concerning end-time events, including the return of Jesus in the book of Revelation.

    For a season of time (over 2,000 years so far), God has allowed the story of Jesus' sacrifice to spread throughout the world giving mankind the opportunity to accept and believe, or reject the Good News (the Gospel) of Jesus' victory.
    At God's appointed time, Jesus will return to gather up all those who have chosen to accept Him as Savior and Lord. He will bring them with Him to be in the presence of God for all eternity. (1 Thess. 4: 15-17)

All those who have failed or refuse to accept God's plan and Jesus' sacrifice are ultimately cast into a place of eternal torment and separation from God's presence (hell).

A slightly deeper look at some of the key events revealed in the Bible helps to explain today's current and approaching events, *and the absolute necessity to make our relationship with God the number one priority of our life.*

In recent years Harrison Ford reportedly addressed the reason for his success in the entertainment industry with, *"You've got to force yourself."* Given all the hindrances, distractions, cares and concerns of life, *"forcing ourselves"* is an absolutely necessary part of "Becoming the Disciple of Truth" that God intends.

Satan, our own self-centered nature, and a world set against the plan and purposes of God will make the reading of this book or the Bible or any of the countless other great Christian books, difficult. **Do not allow yourself to be deterred.** For your own sake and the betterment of all those in your sphere of influence, glean all you can from this book. ***"Force yourself"*** to become the spiritual warrior that God created you to be.

"And you shall know the truth, and the truth shall make you free."
John 8:32 (NKJV)

Becoming a Disciple of Truth

INTRODUCTION

Becoming a Disciple of Truth was written to give anyone an easy and accurate introduction to biblical Christianity. It's a user-friendly and interesting resource guide for those new to Christianity, for mature Christians and everyone in between.

God has always existed. Man finds it easy to study history and envision time going forward into eternity, but to imagine God as having no beginning eludes man's finite understanding. The following pages will not help you understand that profound mystery, however they may help you better understand God's plan of reconciliation with mankind from a historical, as well as from a spiritual perspective.

An old American Indian tale speaks of a grandfather addressing the good vs. evil aspect of human nature with his grandson. It illustrates our human inner conflict and can help to enhance our spiritual understanding.

The grandfather explained to his grandson that within all men, it's as if spirit wolves struggle to control the life of the man. The good wolf wants to do good and help others, while the bad wolf wants only to do that which is selfish and self-serving and at times even evil, without care or concern for others.

As the grandson pondered his grandfather's words, he asked the question, *"Grandfather, which wolf inside me wins?"* Then came wisdom from the grandfather as he said, *"That depends on which one you feed."*

The way we feed the good side of our spirit-nature is by seeking and being in the presence of God, worshipping, meditating, praying and studying the Word of God (the Bible). The Scriptures say, *"People do not live by bread alone, but by every word that comes from the mouth of God."* Matt 4:4 (NLT)

Other ways we "feed" the good side of our spirit-nature is to open ourselves to godly influences such as spending time with good Christian friends, attending church, watching Christian programs, reading God-focused books, listening to Christian radio and helping others.

We feed the bad or self-centered side of our nature by feasting on the non-godly, worldly influences around us. These influences can be found in inappropriate movies and internet sites, books, music, television, drugs, over-indulging in drinking, gambling and spending time with those who pull us away from God. There may be other activities such as work, hobbies, sports, cell phones, etc., that can take so much of our time that we neglect spending time with God.

Much like in the old Indian wolf tale, we as Christians become the person formed by which side of our inner-nature we feed. Pastor Dino Griffin said it like this, "Each man's Soul (thoughts, feelings and will) masquerades as the Spirit, until it comes into alignment with the Spirit of God." Hopefully this book, along with all the other ways God is trying to get your attention, will play a part in transforming you into the spiritual warrior that God created you to be.

Question: Which "wolf" have you been feeding?

Points to consider:
You will encounter two main adversaries to your reading and finishing this book, the enemy camp and your own self-centered nature. Neither of these two wants to relinquish control. **Embrace a sense of urgency** concerning reading this book, because time is slipping away and all the people in your life you care about need you to become the committed disciple God created you to be.

"I beseech you therefore, brethren, by the mercies of God, that you present your bodies a living sacrifice, holy, acceptable to God, which is your reasonable service. And do not be conformed to this world, but be transformed by the renewing of your mind, that you may prove what is that good and acceptable and perfect will of God." Romans 12:1-2 (NKJV)

CHAPTER ONE
THE WAR BEGINS

As described in the Word of God in the book of Revelation, there was a rebellion in the spiritual realm that resulted in the fall of Satan.

"This great dragon -- the ancient serpent called the Devil, or Satan, the one deceiving the whole world -- was thrown down to the earth with all his angels." Rev. 12:9 (NLT)

"His tail dragged down one-third of the stars, which he threw to the earth." Rev. 12:4 (NLT)

One third of the angels liked Satan's challenge that *"You don't have to do what God wants you to do; you can do what you want to do."* To a certain extent that is true. God did not force those angel-followers of Satan to stay in heaven, nor does He over-ride man's free will. Because of pride and rebellion, Satan and his angels were cast out of heaven and will ultimately be cast into a specially prepared place for them called *"The Lake of Fire."*

"Then the Devil, who betrayed them, was thrown into the lake of fire that burns with sulfur, joining the beast and the false prophet. There they will be tormented day and night forever and ever." Revelation 20:10 (NLT)

Against the backdrop of this unfolding spiritual rebellion, God created man.

The Bible spans approximately 6,000 years of man's time on earth. We know that in the first book of the Bible (Genesis) Satan was present in the Garden of Eden. His intention was to spread the rebellion he had started in heaven to newly created mankind (Adam and Eve). He enticed them with the same basic temptation that he used on the angels who followed him. He inferred that man does not have to do what God wants him to do; that man can do what he wants to do.

God gave a very direct command to Adam concerning the garden. *"And the Lord God commanded the man, saying, "Of every tree of the garden you may freely eat; but of the tree of the knowledge of good and evil you shall not eat, for in the day that you eat of it you shall surely die."* **Gen 2:16-17 (NKJV)**

After this, Satan tempted Eve. *"The woman was convinced. The fruit looked so fresh and delicious, and it would make her so wise! So she ate some of the fruit. She also gave some to her husband, who was with her. Then he ate it, too. At that moment, their eyes were opened, and they suddenly felt shame at their nakedness. So they strung fig leaves together around their hips to cover themselves."* Gen. 3:6-7 (NLT)

Adam and Eve listened to the devil and disobeyed God's command not to eat of the fruit of the tree of the knowledge of good and evil.

Satan's motive and obsession to distract or deceive mankind into disobeying God is born of his own pride and his hatred of God. God's offer to mankind includes eternal life in His presence. This, Satan lost when he rebelled against God. In fact, Satan was one of the most powerful angels in heaven, yet he wanted to be like the Most High God. He lusted for the glory that belongs only to God. Satan (called Lucifer or the devil) saw himself rising above the throne of God.

"For you said to yourself, 'I will ascend to heaven and set my throne above God's stars. I will preside on the mountain of the gods far away in the north. I will climb to the highest heavens and be like the Most High.'" Isaiah 14:13-14 (NLT)

Infected by this prideful rebellion and sin, Adam and Eve were cast out of the Garden of Eden, but not without hope. Even though Satan had gained man's authority on earth and successfully tainted man's relationship with God, God had a plan. In the Old Testament book of Genesis 3, verse 15 God foretold of Satan's ultimate demise and man's eventual restoration with Him.

This prophecy by God foretold Satan's "wounding of Jesus' heel" (the future crucifixion of Jesus), and Jesus' victory over Satan, sin and death (Jesus' sacrificial death and resurrection), as "bruising Satan's head."

We may be living in the season of Jesus' final victory over Satan and the rescue of Jesus' believers/followers/disciples; the very ones who will be in God's presence for all eternity.

Questions:

1. How did Satan deceive and tempt Eve?

2. In what ways does man "compete" with God or try to be like Him?

3. What tactic or scheme does Satan use to try to tempt you?

Point to consider:

"Your spiritual effectiveness is proportional to your commitment, sacrifice and continuous pursuit of God's presence, purpose and power."

"On the day that you totally sell out to God and not hold anything back, everything changes."
M.C.

CHAPTER TWO
PRIDE, THE STUMBLING BLOCK

Mankind was not exempt from the effect of pride in the Garden of Eden, and ever since has been continually enticed by prides allure. Over the centuries man has progressed in many areas and become prideful over his accomplishments, to the point that belief and dependence on God has been replaced by dependence on man. Even the perception of the hereafter has been transformed into a false imagined reality.

According to the modernistic teachings of humanistic ideology (humanism), the truth as revealed in the Bible has been deemed inaccurate and irrelevant.

The truth is, everyone who has ever lived will enter into an eternity of unending joy, peace and purpose in God's presence (heaven) **or** into an unending eternity of regret, torment and separation from God (hell).

Failure to adequately understand the great spiritual battle that rages just beyond our physical perception places us in danger of forfeiting our chance of spending eternity with God in heaven. We also risk failing to fulfill our God-ordained purpose of helping others to reach heaven.

Everything we know about God, our existence, the spiritual realm and the physical universe comes from what God has revealed to us by His Spirit and through His Word, the Bible. Though many scientists might like to differ with that statement by referencing all the discoveries, inventions and technologies of man, they are actually taking credit that is not theirs to take.

For example, man prides himself in all that he has been able to accomplish in harnessing the power of hydraulics. Using this so-called discovery, man can move and lift tremendous amounts of weight, build roads and skyscrapers, and dig his way through mountains. But, they are doing little more than accessing the same power and technology that God orchestrated and "invented" when He created spiders. It is through the use of hydraulics that spiders raise and move their legs. Yet, modern man thinks and acts as though he is responsible for the "invention and creation" of this very useful technology.

A similar example of man's prideful misconception of his wisdom and creative genius is in the harnessing of nuclear power. With it we power our cities, our warships, and can even kill thousands of people with a single detonation. In movies it is the usual "go to" weapon when man is confronted with upheavals of nature, oppressive military forces, and even to fend off alien attacks. Oh how clever man considers himself at having discovered or created nuclear power.

Man marvels at what he has been able to accomplish by splitting the atom, while God uses nuclear fission and fusion to fuel the stars to give off their heat and brightness across the universe.

In all these cases, it is actually man stumbling across physical laws that God has created and designed, or God intentionally giving ideas to man by way of dreams and visions. (see 2010 post by Man from Modesto)

That some men fail to see and revere the real architect of the universe is a clear example of the following verse, *"For since the creation of the world His* (God's) *invisible attributes are clearly seen, being understood by the things that are made, even His eternal power and Godhead, so that they are without excuse, because, although they knew God, they did not glorify Him as God, nor were thankful, but became futile in their thoughts, and their foolish hearts were darkened.* **Professing to be wise, they became fools, . . .**" Romans 1:20-22 (NKJV)

The intricacies, complexities and massiveness of the physical universe tend to influence our initial perception of the spiritual realm as a lesser "smoke and vapor" realm of little substance. Movies and television have helped to produce this subordinate perception of the spiritual realm, when in reality this physical earthly world that seems so real and so concrete, is actually temporary.

The spiritual realm has dominion over this earthly physical realm and will continue to exist long after the light of the sun of our solar system fades into oblivion.

The historical records and stories reported throughout the Bible are not "stand alone" events. They were specifically designed by God and passed down through the generations as a way to guide people in all aspects of their lives. More so than people of today's generation realize, many of these stories have targeted application to the prophesied end-time age. The entire world is starting to see this unfold.

A clear understanding of how God is controlling these converging current end-time events will help people to avoid fear, and to know how to have confidence, while acting with purpose and love.

Question:
   1. In what ways has man taken God for granted and become prideful by giving credit for his successes, to himself?

Point to consider:
   True Disciples of Christ **must constantly re-align** their focus onto spiritual understanding and not allow the distractions of the physical and spiritual realm to dissuade or diminish the God-aligned plan and purpose that God intends for their life.

"Since, then, you have been raised with Christ, set your hearts on things above, where Christ is, seated at the right hand of God. Set your minds on things above, not on earthly things." Colossians 3:1-2 (NKJV)

CHAPTER THREE
MAN STRUGGLES / GOD RESTORES

Reconciliation with God happens when individuals recognize their separation from God, repent (turn away) from their sins and accept Jesus' death and sacrifice as the only acceptable and sufficient payment for their sins.

Salvation is not a matter of a simple prayer that someone says and then returns to living just the way they did before saying the prayer. This prayer must contain **a heart-felt regret** for having lived a prideful, self-centered life of disbelief, rebellion and sin. It requires **repentance,** or turning away from sin and from those things that are displeasing to God. It should also include a commitment to **wholeheartedly follow Jesus.** (2 Corinthians 7:10)

This decision results in an increased awareness and a growing sense of reverence and respect for God referred to as "fear of the Lord."

"Fear of the LORD is the beginning of knowledge. Only fools despise wisdom and discipline." Prov. 1:7 (NLT)

God does not and will not look upon sin with any degree of endorsement. God made man to fellowship with Him, but that fellowship was broken because of sin. Jesus, our Messiah and Savior, fulfilled God's plan of redemption when

God sent Jesus to earth as a man to die on the cross for all of mankind's sins.

When we declare and accept Jesus' sacrifice we make Him our Savior and Lord. This requires repentance, loyalty and obedience to Him. In so doing, we become destined to live eternally in heaven with God.

In the Old Testament of the Bible God required blood sacrifices (ex. unblemished lambs) to atone or to provide temporary payment for sin. In so doing, He was preparing mankind to understand the nature of Jesus' future blood sacrifice.

It is because of the innocent shed blood of Jesus that all of mankind's sins have been forgiven or remitted.

"For the wages of sin is death, but the free gift of God is eternal life through Christ Jesus our Lord." Romans 6:23 (NLT)

"In fact, according to the law of Moses, nearly everything was purified with blood. For **without the shedding of blood, there is no forgiveness.***"* Heb. 9:22 (NLT)

Because of Jesus' shed blood and sacrificial death and resurrection, a way back to a right relationship with God the Father was made for all mankind.

"For God so loved the world that he gave his only Son, so that everyone who believes in him will not perish but have eternal life. God did

not send his Son into the world to condemn it, but to save it." John 3:16-17 (NLT)

The decision to ask for God's forgiveness, the acceptance of the gift of Jesus' shed blood, death and resurrection, and the subsequent sincere actions of serving and following Jesus, results in a changed life. The old nature passes away and a person becomes a new creation and no longer habitually continues in the behaviors of his former self-centered and sinful life.

In addition to the physical birth we all experience, a believer experiences a second "spiritual birthing" into the family of God.

"Jesus answered, "Most assuredly, I say to you, unless one is born of water and the Spirit, he cannot enter the kingdom of God. That which is born of the flesh is flesh, and that which is born of the Spirit is spirit." John 3:5-6 (NKJV)

As with the early disciples, every "saved" person who accepts Jesus as their Lord and Savior is given a mandate by God to become an active player on His side, and to be a witness for the Good News of Jesus Christ's victory.

And Jesus came and spoke to them, saying, "All authority has been given to Me in heaven and on earth. Go therefore and make disciples of all the nations, baptizing them in the name of the Father and of the Son and of the Holy Spirit, teaching them to observe all things that I have commanded you; and lo, I am with you always, even to the end of the age." Mt. 28:18-20 (NKJV)

In this current age of technology, creature comforts and the plethora of entertainment options that distract us, functioning as an effective disciple of Christ is a difficult path. Many Christians can be better described as "fair-weather Christians."

When things begin to get a little difficult or when their Christian walk starts to cost them something, many "professing" believers begin to hold back on their Christian responsibilities. They don't do all they could or should do to further the cause of Christ. They may become apathetic in their Christian resolve and slip into more comfortable *"surely someone else like the pastor, or the bible study leader, or the televangelist, or whoever else will reach these people. Besides, they are probably better and much more able to reach them that I am"* mindset.

The truth is that the forces of the enemy are playing an all-out battle for the souls of men while many in the professing Christian body treat these life-and-death issues like a hobby. In order to counteract the unrelenting attack of the enemy in this regard, a believer must be **intentional and very deliberate** regarding his or her responsibility to help Jesus in His mission to **"destroy the works of the devil".** 1 John 3:8

While this book provides a significant amount of helpful information, its design, purpose and intent is that the reader become willing to follow Christ in a ***very intentional and deliberate way.***

This will be a costly adventure. It will require time spent pursuing a strong and growing relationship with the Lord. The forces of darkness, the demands of your job, hobbies, family and friends, and your own self-centered fleshly nature may hinder your many well-intended steps. **Do not yield to the pressure and distractions of life.**

Do not put off attending that bible study or upcoming revival event or fail to finish reading this book, or any other spiritually encouraging book. God is trying to impact your life in a variety of ways. Fight the temptation to resist His pursuit of you.

*"Wrestle not against the plan
and purposes of God."*

Yielding to worldly distractions results in the weakening of our own spiritual walk and the diminishing of the influence we can be in the lives of friends and loved ones. The self-awareness of one's shallow commitment to Christ increases their feeling of unworthiness to approach God about prayerful concerns. This weakens their expectance to see God answer their prayers. Shallow faith and lack of commitment or lack of effort creates doubt in the mind. Doubt and unbelief are the enemies of faith.

"But without faith it is impossible to please Him, for he who comes to God must believe that He is, and that He is a rewarder of those who diligently seek Him." Hebrews 11:6 (NKJV)

This book is designed to help you become the **intentional and very deliberate Christian** all those around you need you to be.

Questions:

1. What steps are necessary to be reconciled with God and to become included in the family of God?
2. What are the distractions in your life that hinder your spiritual growth and connection with God's people?
3. How can your pursuit of God become more intentional and deliberate?

Points to consider:

The forces of darkness are committed and relentless in their effort to undermine the purposes and plans of God. Effective Christians must likewise be totally committed and yielded to the leading of the Holy Spirit of God in the great spiritual battle that rages. Do not allow pride or complacency to sabotage your calling and your effectiveness.

Remember Jesus said, *"I am the vine, you are the branches. He who abides in Me, and I in him, bears much fruit;* **for without Me you can do nothing.***"* John 15:5 (NKJV)

CHAPTER FOUR
CHRISTIANITY vs. OTHER RELIGIONS

Christianity differs from all other religions on earth in some profound ways. In many of the world's other mainstream religions, the way to heaven, paradise, nirvana, etc. involves man becoming better or somehow working his way to heaven, or reincarnating and attaining a higher level of existence.

In Christianity, it is not about what we do or have done that allows us to earn our way to God. **It is and always will be about what Jesus did.** He came down from heaven and willingly sacrificed Himself to pay for our sin and rebellion.

When Jesus said in John 19:30, *"It is finished: and He bowed His head, and gave up the ghost,"* He completed the one and only sacrifice necessary for the remission of anyone's sins if they truly repent and ask for forgiveness. His sacrifice was the final sacrifice forever, for the forgiveness of all sins. Never again would any sacrifice be needed to atone or make up for the sins of man.

Because of Jesus' sacrificial death man cannot become prideful over "earning" his way to heaven. In having structured man's reconciliation with Him through Jesus, God dealt with the pride issue of mankind for all eternity.

"God saved you by his grace when you believed. And you can't take credit for this; it is a

gift from God. Salvation is not a reward for the good things we have done, so none of us can boast about it." Eph. 2:8-9 (NLT)

Compared with many other belief systems, Christianity deals extensively with the sinful nature of man and the evil influences of the devil and his demons in the spiritual realm. Most other religions gloss over or fail to address the destructive nature of man's own self-centered and prideful nature as well as the tactics of man's adversary, the devil.

Because most other religions do not adequately address man's sin; they do not stress man's need of a Savior. Contrary to the misguided hope, belief and teachings of many, there is a real place of torment and eternal separation from God called hell. God spoke often throughout the Bible about this place of eternal torment to warn man and also entire nations.

"The wicked shall be turned into hell, And all the nations that forget God."
Psalms 9:17 (NKJV)

Some professing Christian groups teach an incorrect and false teaching that Jesus is just an angel or that Jesus and Lucifer are brothers. One mainstream Christian denomination teaches that the works and rituals of those still living can atone or pay for the wrong doing (sin) of a departed loved one. Another group believes and teaches that the living can perform a baptism for the benefit of a loved one who has died and was not baptized when they were alive.

Among the non-Christian religions, probably the most successful, anti-true God religion is the religion of Islam. Since the inception of this cleverly and demonically devised counterfeit religion some 600 years after Jesus walked the earth, Islam has been able to deceive and enslave over one billion people on the planet. (More about this in chapters 25 – 27).

There is an ongoing debate on the correct name of Jesus to be used in writing, reference and prayer. Many are used to the English version, "Jesus." Throughout the world, the name "Jesus" has many different variations based on the regional language of well over 100 different countries or nations. Some Christian theologians teach and prefer to use the Hebrew derivative Greek word "Yeshua" in writings and when used in prayer. They believe that referring to or addressing "Jesus" as "Yeshua" is more accurate and better correlates to the actual name of "Jesus" according to the Greek translation of His Hebrew name. The use of the name Yeshua, as well as any of the other regional variations are absolutely okay, as long as the One being referenced or prayed in the name of, is the living Son of the living God who died on the cross for the sins of mankind and subsequently rose from the dead. He (Jesus, Yeshua, etc.) is great enough to understand and accept our sincere effort to revere and honor Him.

Question:

>   1. What is the most successful false religion on the planet?

>   2. How does one achieve "salvation"?

Points to consider:

The most significant difference between Christianity and all other religions is that **in no other religion or belief system did the creator, leader or central figure of that religion, die in order to pay for the sin nature of man and then rise again from the dead.**

The committed and effective disciple of Christ will encounter much resistance, including resistance from within the "professing" body of Christ. Remember, *"you can't debate someone into the family of God but you can love them into the kingdom."* Love has no limitation and is the ultimate weapon of our warfare.

CHAPTER FIVE
THE FLAWED ATHEIST'S PERSPECTIVE

As scientists explore the world and the universe that surrounds us, a recurring pattern of order and balance is discovered. There are opposites in most everything that exists. There is heat and there is cold. There is light and there is darkness. There is good and there is evil. Everything that exists in the physical universe (including aliens if they exist) or in the spiritual realm, were made by God.

"In the beginning was the Word, and the Word was with God, and the Word was God. He was in the beginning with God. All things were made through Him, **and without Him nothing was made that was made.** *In Him was life, and the life was the light of men. And the light shines in the darkness, and the darkness did not comprehend it."* John 1:1-5 (NKJV)

The atheist believes in neither the Kingdom of God nor His adversary's dominion, the kingdom of darkness ruled by Satan. One simple and easy way to grasp the existence of God is found in the following "watch story."

Imagine an intricately made and carefully crafted Swiss watch - not some new technology, electronically-driven timepiece, but rather a pre-electronic-age device with many moving parts and spring assemblies.

Now imagine that you totally disassemble the watch and place all of the loose pieces in a small box. Next, imagine that you shake all the pieces around in the box for several seconds and then stop to look at the condition of the watch in the box. It remains just a bunch of pieces in chaotic disarray. Shake the box for several seconds more and stop to examine the contents of the box. Again, what you will see is just a bunch of disorganized watch parts in a box.

You repeat the process over and over again, always stopping to check the status of the watch. According to statistics, one in some XX billions of times of shaking the box, you will find the watch assembled and running in perfect order.

Even the atheist knows that while statistics suggest that one in some huge number of shakings will result in the watch assembling itself, it just isn't going to happen. The question for the atheist then becomes, "How can you understand that this watch will never assemble itself and begin to run in perfect order, and yet you believe that the earth and universe somehow just assembled itself (with all newly created parts from nothing) and is running in perfect order?

The answer is that the earth did not statistically just happen on its own. It was the Creator God who designed and made from nothing this place we call earth. *"The fool has said in his heart, "There is no God."* Psalms 14:1 (NKJV)

I once heard an old preacher tell a story about the learned scientists of earth challenging

God, claiming that they could create life apart from God. First God sprinkled some dirt on the ground and then breathed onto the dirt and that dust became a living soul. Then the scientists got ready to fabricate their effort and brought in several buckets of dirt which they spread over the laboratory floor. Then God spoke and said, *"Oh no, get your own dirt."*

Evidence attesting to the existence of God is the Bible itself. Though not considered a science book by mainstream modern educators, we see modern science corroborates what the Bible has said all along.

In the area of geography, modern discoveries by geologists and archeologists continue to confirm what the Bible has said for centuries. Modern day discoveries of the ruins of ancient cities and artifacts written about in the Bible help confirm the historical record and attest to the authenticity of the Bible.

Across the broad spectrum of physical sciences and historical studies, the Bible is continually proving to be accurate. Bible skeptics discount all the affirming evidence found in modern day scientific and historical discoveries as mere coincidence. There is however, something about the Bible that they have a great deal of difficulty discarding as coincidence. It actually comes from what was one of their strongest arguments against Biblical Christianity.

The anti-Bible scoffer's argument against the authenticity of the Bible hinged on all of the end-time prophecies concerning Israel. For centuries they were quick to point out that Israel ceased to exist as a nation around 70 A.D. when Jerusalem was destroyed by the Romans and the Jews were displaced. Since that time, the Jews were scattered throughout the world. The end-time prophecies about Israel (that did not technically exist as a nation for centuries), was proof to them that the Bible was blatantly wrong, and therefore the prophesy, false.

Those anti-Bible proponents became curiously silent when, out of the ashes of World War II Israel re-emerged as a nation on May 14th 1948. Since that date, the Star of David has continually flown over the nation Israel. God has been true to His Word and has been gathering His people back to Israel ever since.

Another prophesied practice from the Bible that has seemed out-of-touch and inconsistent with man's progress attained in the modern era, is the barbarous act of beheading people. In the Bible book of Revelation, the beheading of people who refuse to renounce their belief in Jesus Christ is prophesied. *"... And I saw the souls of those who had been beheaded for their testimony about Jesus and for proclaiming the word of God..."* Rev. 20:4 (NLT)

This practice that seemed so antiquated and so Old Testament has re-emerged as the "go-to" act of Islamic terrorism in their jihad (Holy War) against Jews, Christians and all non-Muslim (infidels) on the planet. This war against God's people is another prophecy being fulfilled right before our eyes.

Islamic terrorists think they are on their god's side (Allah) in killing God's people (Jews) and all non-Muslims. Jesus said, *". . . yes, the time is coming that whoever kills you will think that he offers God service. And these things they will do to you because they have not known the Father nor me. But these things I have told you, that when the time comes, you may remember that I told you of them."* John 16:2-3 (NKJV)

This, as well as other current signs indicating the imminent end-time conflict, should give anyone paying attention sufficient reason to very seriously consider the true state of their relationship with the Lord.

God's son Jesus, revealed God's plan of reconciliation first to the Jews (Israel), and then through His disciples to the whole world (Gentiles). God extends to all mankind the opportunity to respect and accept the sacrifice of Jesus on the cross to pay for their sins. This opened the door for man to become **"saved"** from the penalty of sin and **adopted into God's family.**

Once adopted, believers are destined to live with God forever. Along with that "saved" reality comes the **responsibility** to help others reach that same saved condition. All believers are called to spread the **gospel** throughout the world and share the story of God's redemptive plan through Jesus' sacrifice. (Matthew 28:19-20)

If someone professes to be a Christian and does not put forth effort to bring others to a saving and intimate relationship with God through Jesus Christ, the reality of their own salvation experience could easily be questioned.

When we really believe and understand the eternal consequences involved, we are compelled to reach those lost in their sin and challenge them to repent and accept Jesus as Savior and Lord.

Disciples of Truth warn the unsaved of the eternal great danger that exists and of the Gospel of Jesus Christ which is their only hope of rescue.

Question:
1. Do you seize opportunities to reach out to others concerning their need to make Jesus the Lord of their lives?

Point to consider: God made every atom, grain of sand and molecule on the planet. He likewise made the sun, planets and moons of our solar system. He made all of the estimated 500 billion stars in our galaxy and the over 500 billion galaxies in the universe. And yet, there are those who refuse to acknowledge, revere, respect and honor Him for who He is, what He's done and the love He has proved toward us, through Jesus Christ. *"Such things ought not be so."*

CHAPTER SIX
THINK YOU MIGHT BE A CHRISTIAN?

Many Christians seem to have a "cross their fingers" hope about their life after death. Sincerely accepting Jesus Christ as Savior and following Him as Lord provides the "assurance of our salvation."

"For if you confess with your mouth that Jesus is Lord and believe in your heart that God raised him from the dead, you will be saved. For it is by believing in your heart that you are made right with God, and it is by confessing with your mouth that you are saved." Romans 10:9-10 (NLT)

Following this faith commitment, there is the challenge of learning to live as Jesus commanded. He did not promise His followers that their walk with Him would always be easy.

"I have told you all this so that you may have peace in me. Here on earth you will have many trials and sorrows. But take heart, because I have overcome the world." John 16:33 (NLT)

"And when He (Jesus) had called the people to Himself, with His disciples also, he said unto them, **"Whosoever desires to come after Me, let him deny himself, and take up his cross, and follow Me."** Mark 8:34 (NKJV)

One of God's promises to man is that He has a plan for each of us. (Jeremiah 29:11) However, man has always been reluctant to say "no" to his own wants and fleshly desires and

repent or turn away from his sin. Following in the path Jesus laid out requires one to be in faith, humble, repentant and unselfish. This can only be accomplished by the power of the Holy Spirit and requires the born-again" experience resulting in a new nature. To repent and deny one's self-centered nature or not, is man's raging inner struggle. It is each person's individual choice.

The apostle Paul spoke of the battle all Christians contend with on a daily basis.

"So I say, let the Holy Spirit guide your lives. Then you won't be doing what your sinful nature craves. The sinful nature wants to do evil, which is just the opposite of what the Spirit wants. And the Spirit gives us desires that are the opposite of what the sinful nature desires. These two forces are constantly fighting each other, so you are not free to carry out your good intentions." Gal. 5:16-17 (NLT)

Each day we choose either to make God and His purpose the priority of our life, or we let our job, fame, money, hobbies, latest national news event, entertainment, health issue or possibly life-controlling habits such as drinking, drugs, pornography, gambling, etc., remain the real priorities and strongholds of our life. When we do this, we often try to "work God in" at some lower level of importance, neglecting to let Him reside in His first and rightful position of honor.

Some may do good works, give money to the church or those in need, serve in a ministry and appear to be in godly right-standing, yet do all this with a self-serving motive. Some may rely on their own talents and gifts, discounting the supernatural power of the Holy Spirit.

"They will act as if they are religious, but they will reject the power that could make them godly. You must stay away from people like that." 2 Tim 3:5 (NLT)

When we surrender our plan for our life and accept God's plan and purpose, we allow God's Holy Spirit (the power of God) to flow through us. When we do this, we are in the "ready" position and at a place where God can and will use us. However, He will not force His will on us. We must learn to partner with God and **put forth the effort to deny our own self-will and actively yield to His.** This is a life-long process.

Consider Jesus' words which can be sobering even to the believer.

"Not all people who sound religious are really godly. **They may refer to me as 'Lord,' but they still won't enter the Kingdom of Heaven.** *The decisive issue is whether they obey my Father in heaven. On judgment day many will tell me, 'Lord, Lord, we prophesied in your name and cast out demons in your name and performed many miracles in your name.' But I will reply, 'I never knew you. Go away;* **the things you did were unauthorized."** Matt. 7:21-23 (NLT)

Ask yourself, *Am I living an unauthorized life? Is what I'm doing each day part of God's plan for my life or am I doing my own thing, my way? Do I "know" the transforming love of God?*

The importance of "knowing God" is nearly impossible to over-stress. Many Christians do a fairly good job of focusing on the Bible and becoming well-versed in it, but is God's Spirit of love transforming them? Without this love it's easy to become "religious" in the same manner as the Pharisees of Jesus' time. The Pharisees were experts on "the letter of the law" but completely missed God's living message of love.

When Christians become solely focused on the Bible and do not develop an intimate relationship with the Lord, they may become judgmental and legalistic in how they walk their walk. This leads to looking at everything and everyone in terms of how others do or do not fulfill the law, which no one can fully. They can become experts at finding fault, but deficient in offering love and forgiveness, failing to tap into grace in the same manner as Jesus did. The Pharisees of Jesus' time were examples of legalistic-minded religion.

Today as "religious legalists" venture into the world, everyone is evaluated in the cold harsh light of the law. What is usually absent in their own personal lives is **the intimacy of an ongoing, two-way conversation** (relationship)

with God. They run the risk of falling into the *"I never knew you"* group (Matt. 7:21-23 NKJV) that Jesus spoke about.

It's a challenge for all Christians to move beyond asking God to fulfill their list of wants and needs, to engaging in intimate and open conversations with Him; the God who created them for fellowship and revelation. Regarding anything less….. *"such things ought not be so."*

Questions all Christians should ask themselves:

How is my intimate conversation/prayer time with God going? Have I tried to make God more like a Santa Clause who makes things come out the way I want them to? Do I display the love of God in me to the world around me?

Strong suggestion: *Get the God-conversation going in your life!*

In no way is this said to diminish the importance of pursuing God through His Word, the Bible. It can be a challenge to initiate or to intensify your "knowing relationship" with the Lord. This requires a yielding each day to the leading of the Holy Spirit.

In God-designed order, both the pursuit of God through His Word and the pursuit of God through an intimate personal relationship with Him will be done together, and not one at the expense of the other.

The truth is, if we want to spend eternity in the presence of God we must initially yield to His leading and force ourselves if need be, to spend time seeking God in the Word and in His presence. The more we do this, the more we will desire His presence and want to express our love for Him. The more someone pursues God, the more serving Him will become a pleasure and become **the priority** of their life.

Questions:
1. What do you need to do on a daily basis to bring your relationship with God into alignment? Write it down, save it and review it often.

Point to consider:
A real Disciple of Truth never forgets, but rather cherishes the fact that he is an ambassador of Christ and is called to fulfill God's ordained purpose for his/her life. Yielding to the Holy Spirit, meditating on the Word of God and seeking God's presence daily develops the kind of relationship necessary to fulfill God's plan for one's life. *" Jesus came and told his disciples, "I have been given all authority in heaven and on earth. Therefore, go and make disciples of all the nations, baptizing them in the name of the Father and the Son and the Holy Spirit. Teach these new disciples to obey all the commands I have given you. And be sure of this: I am with you always, even to the end of the age."* Matt. 28:18-20

CHAPTER SEVEN
CHRISTIANS AND LOOK-A-LIKES
(Who is really saved?)

Before too long and even if it's only in our own mind we can find ourselves questioning,

"Is he really saved? How can he be saved when he does the things he does? They "profess" to be Christians, but somehow something doesn't seem to be right. Am I really saved?"

How do you know? When it comes down to others, we don't know. That is between each person and God. The issue revolves around what an individual **really believes** and whether they made the decision to accept Jesus' sacrifice, resurrection and Lordship.

A salesman who does well usually spends a considerable amount of time educating himself to the point of **knowing** the product or service he is promoting. What if an unforeseen flaw or weakness in the product comes to his attention? Does he change jobs or change product lines because he can no longer in good conscience promote or sell the product(s) or service? He has a decision to make **because he no longer believes** in what he is selling.

In this world of many "professing Christians" and this *we tend to promote what we really believe in* characteristic, the degree to which a believer brings the Gospel of Jesus Christ to others is a strong indicator as to the degree to which someone really believes in Christianity.

When an appliance salesman seems reluctant to spend time or expend much effort in selling a particular product to us, we sense that he does not have confidence in his product, and maybe neither should we. When a professing Christian is not enthusiastic and actively trying to guide the unsaved to Christ, we sense that he does not have confidence in his product (Christianity), and maybe neither should others.

Many professing Christians are engaged in, concerned about and with a right motive, doing something about the salvation of others. Other professing Christians may say a lot of well-sounding things but are not really doing anything of consequence about the salvation of others. Their motives may come into question.

What someone is actually doing about reaching the unsaved reveals much about what they really believe about Christianity. **It is nearly impossible to be a committed, strong believer in Christ, and not be actively praying and doing something about the salvation of others.**

The "really saved" aspect of Christianity is important when we examine our own lives. In many churches the focus is on getting someone to make a profession of faith, or sometimes referred to as a decision for Christ. Often a group or organization keeps track of how many salvations (professions or decisions) are made in a particular service, revival or event. Unfortunately in their zeal to record many salvations, the necessity of really **believing and repenting** is not adequately emphasized.

Inadvertently, though usually with good intentions, some churches are getting professions of faith but not necessarily true believing and repenting salvations. Many of those who fall into this "professing-only" category have a shallow attitude of, *"Oh, all I have to do is say that I accept Jesus and I get to go to heaven? Sure I'll do that!"* Satan couldn't be happier with this deception. (More about this in Chapter 24.)

In addition to the multitudes of unsaved individuals that need to be reached outside the church, there are vast numbers of "confessing-only" Christians within the church that need to be challenged to a greater level of belief, repentance, prayer and a genuine reliance on God and His power which is available to all believers.

"For indeed the gospel was preached to us as well as to them; but the word which they heard did not profit them, ***not being mixed with faith*** *in those who heard it."* Heb. 4:2 (NKJV)

Refusing to "see" our own weaknesses and being resistant to repentant of our sinful tendencies prevents us from developing an intimate, "knowing" relationship with God. Moving from a casual lukewarm relationship with the Lord to an intimate relationship where one fully embraces Jesus and His mission to reach the world is every disciple's challenge.

Many of the confession-only professions of faith were based on a salvation prayer that may not have been heart-felt. The essential **believing** and **repenting** components were never brought to fruition.

The key indicator of true salvation is whether someone's life has really changed. Have they abandoned their old selfish desires, their ways of thinking and acting to become a **committed Disciple of Jesus Christ?**

True salvation results in a passion that compels a believer to take risks to spread the gospel (Good News of Jesus' victory). This kind of passion requires that one fully embrace what Jesus did because of love. Yielding to the power of the Holy Spirit in prayer and in daily activities, plus the pursuit of the Word of God will transform the believer. (Romans 12: 1-2)

Each person must ask himself if his motivation is "God aligned" or does his belief move him to serve in a particular ministry out of a sense of duty, the desire to be noticed, to acquire a certain position or simply to please or impress someone else. Each individual believer must choose whether to follow and pursue God's plan or to follow and pursue man's plan of ministry.

Some of today's church leaders and even some pastors may not be in a right, God-aligned relationship with the Lord. They may yield to the ever-present temptation to back away from stressing the need of repentance that results in changing behavior for fear of losing members.

Jesus said, *"No, and I tell you again that unless you repent, you will perish, too."* Luke 13:5 (NLT)

Too important not to say again!

Jesus said, *"No, and I tell you again that unless you repent, you will perish, too."* Luke 13:5 (NLT)

While most pastors, teachers and leaders do care about others, some preach well-sounding, non-confrontational, morality-based messages but speak little about the cross, repentance, the shed blood of Jesus or the importance of each individual's responsibility to spread the Good News of Jesus Christ's victory over sin and death.

To clarify what all believers are to do, Jesus gave to all generations what is called **The Great Commission**,

"Go therefore and make disciples of all the nations, baptizing them in the name of the Father and of the Son and of the Holy Spirit, teaching them to observe all things that I have commanded you; and lo, I am with you always, even to the end of the age. Amen." Matthew 28:19-20 (NKJV)

God gives instructions and fair-warning to many in the church today who are putting their trust in a repent-less, non-intimate, non-God-knowing type of religion. *"Not everyone who calls out to me, 'Lord! Lord!' will enter the*

Kingdom of Heaven. ***Only those who actually do the will of my Father in heaven will enter.*** *On judgment day many will say to me, 'Lord! Lord! We prophesied in your name and cast out demons in your name and performed many miracles in your name.'* ***But I will reply, 'I never knew you. Get away from me, you who break God's laws.'"*** Matt. 7:21-23 (NLT)

Questions:
1. Have you repented and turned away from those things that you know are displeasing to God in order that God's will and plan for your life might take preeminence?
2. If not, write down your plan for doing something about it; then do it!

Point to consider:

In this world of many "professing Christians" and this *"we tend to promote what we really believe in"* characteristic, the degree to which a believer brings the gospel of Jesus Christ to others in word and deed, is a strong indicator as to the degree to which someone really believes in Christianity.

The completion of repentance results in:
1) faith that you have been forgiven, and
2) the love of God that you desire to share
   with others.

CHAPTER EIGHT
HEAVEN IS OPTIONAL

Many will miss heaven because they do not "know Jesus" in a personal and intimate way as they continue to spend their lives focusing on the cares and concerns of this present world. Some who profess to be Christians may look like they are in a saved relationship with the Lord, but in fact they are not.

By some estimates nearly 50% of those attending Christian-named churches, may not really be saved and living in a right relationship with the Lord. They are much like an artificial tree branch that is attached to a living tree. It looks like part of the tree**, but since it is not in a living, life-flow relationship with the tree it does not produce any fruit.**

Jesus said, *"Yes, I am the vine; you are the branches. Those who remain in me, and I in them, will produce much fruit.* ***For apart from me you can do nothing."*** John 15:5 (NLT)

True Christianity is based on a changed heart filled with the love of God and reflecting His character. (Romans 12:2) The relationship a person has with God through Jesus Christ results in loving and forgiving others. The nature of God within us (the power of the Holy Spirit) enables us to do this. Talking like a Christian is not proof positive of being a Christian. Acting toward others as Jesus did, turning away from sin and helping others do the same, are much better indicators of a true disciple of Christ.

Jesus said, *"So now I am giving you a new commandment: Love each other. Just as I have loved you, you should love each other.* ***Your love for one another will prove to the world that you are my disciples."*** John 13:34-35 (NLT)

Today is the day of salvation. There is only one way to get in a right relationship with God. Jesus said to him, *"I am the way,* ***the truth****, and the life. No one comes to the Father except through Me."* John 14:6 (NKJV)

"Nor is there salvation in any other, for there is no other name under heaven given among men by which we must be saved." Acts 4:12 (NKJV)

Some of today's most prominent spiritual, political and public figures believe there are many ways to God's presence in heaven, yet they are tragically mistaken. The influence of their words and the result of their deceitful teaching will, for those trusting in these false teachers, play a part in their eternal separation from God.

The Bible tells us about a book found in heaven called the **Lamb's Book of Life.** In it are the names of those who are destined to spend eternity with God. Anyone who does not accept Jesus as Savior nor obey Him as Lord will be destined to suffer the same eternal fate as Satan. *"And anyone whose name was not found*

recorded in the Book of Life was thrown into the lake of fire."
Rev. 20:15 (NLT)

As Bible prophecy is fulfilled and the end-times quickly approach, we all should ask, ***"Is my name in the book? Are the names of my friends, family and other loved ones in the book?***

We are not promised tomorrow and may actually have little time left on earth. Sadly, some who are reading this book may delay making a decision to accept Jesus as their Savior and Lord. An unexpected death or the Lord's return would eliminate their chance of going to heaven. In addition, delaying the decision to accept Jesus also weakens the godly influence one could have in the lives of those they care about.

Because of the constant worldly pressure to ignore God's commands, many have fallen into sinful behaviors such as becoming sexually active outside the bounds of marriage, or the "living-together trap" that in so many ways seems so convenient, logical and in these modern times, acceptable. There may be times when due to unusual circumstances or forces of economic stress couples find themselves residing under the same roof. In these types of situations they can easily begin engaging in an intimate sexual relationship outside the bounds of marriage. They may even be in the early stages of going to a church and becoming more aware of the commands of God. Even though they may be drawing closer to embracing God in many ways, their ongoing sexual relationship continues to be a problem that must **not** be ignored.

This behavior is further complicated by the clever whisperings of the enemy who says, *"Hey, what's the big deal, you've been doing these kinds of things for some time now and you plan to get married, right?"* Whether involved in ungodly sexual behavior or a plethora of other seemingly acceptable behaviors (according to current social norms), individuals often do not realize the danger they are in of finding themselves eternally separated from God.

"Don't you realize that those who do wrong will not inherit the Kingdom of God? Don't fool yourselves. **Those who indulge in sexual sin, or who worship idols, or commit adultery, or are male prostitutes, or practice homosexuality, or are thieves, or greedy people, or drunkards, or are abusive, or cheat people— none of these will inherit the Kingdom of God. Some of you were once like that. But you were cleansed;** *you were made holy; you were made right with God by calling on the name of the Lord Jesus Christ and by the Spirit of our God."* 1 Cor. 6:9-11 (NLT)

Should someone find themselves in the position of trying to honor God's call for sexual purity until marriage, yet are currently "living with someone" and have been sexually intimate outside the bounds of marriage, there is but one thing to do. Repent immediately. Until separate living accommodations can be made or until they are officially married, all sexually intimate behavior should cease. **Period.**

1 Corinthians 6: 9-11 gives a clear warning to the consequences of sin. Each person should prayerfully evaluate his/her own life. Beliefs and behaviors of the professing Christian should line up with God's Word. All ungodly beliefs and behaviors should not be justified, but rather terminated especially those clearly identified in these verses. There are many people who never fully contemplate these verses or somehow determine these condemned behaviors don't apply to them, or they believe the "goodness" of God somehow exempts them from being held accountable. **NEWSFLASH – These verses apply to you as well as everyone else on the planet.**

God has been very clear about these things. Furthermore, *"God is not a man, that He should lie, Nor a son of man, that He should repent. Has He said, and will He not do? Or has He spoken, and will He not make it good."* Numbers 23:19 (NKJV)

God's love embraces all of us where we are, but God is not content with leaving us in an estranged state. His love compels us to move out and away from any behavior that could exclude us from attaining His heavenly presence.

Personal opinions, societal norms or laws designed by man do not over-rule the Word of God. If the behaviors identified in these verses concern you, repent and turn away from them lest they cost you heaven.

Establish your right relationship with God and **be confident about where you will spend eternity now,** while there is still time. Then do all you can to help others come to Christ, enabling them to enter into the eternal presence of God.

God promises that He has a perfect plan for each of us. *"For I know the plans I have for you," says the* LORD. *"They are plans for good and not for disaster, to give you a future and a hope. In those days when you pray, I will listen.* ***If you look for me wholeheartedly, you will find me."*** Jeremiah 29:11-13 (NLT)

Question:

1. Is your name in the Lamb's Book of Life?

Point to consider:

True Christianity transforms one's mind, heart, and behavior in a manner that reflects His character. (Romans 12:2) The nature of God within us (the power of the Holy Spirit) enables us to love and forgive others. Talking like a Christian is not proof positive of being a Christian. Acting toward others as Jesus did, turning away from sin, and helping others do the same are much better indicators of a true Disciple of Christ.

CHAPTER NINE
ADVERSITY'S SILVER LINING

Satan uses adversity in people's lives to cause them to despair, become angry at God and distance themselves from Him. God allows adversity in people's lives because in actuality, it is often adversity that brings people to the end of themselves. This is also the point where people often become more open to and ready to turn to God.

When things are going well people tend to rely on their own success, wealth, fame or abilities. Few people turn to God when they are living in a state of great worldly success. The vast majority of genuine salvations occur when sufficient adversity (job loss, divorce, loss of a loved one, a health crisis, financial difficulty, disaster, etc.) brings us to the point where we realize we need God.

There are many ways people can respond to the Gospel of Jesus Christ. There are those who hear a pastor's message and feel the inward pull of God's love and right then and there accept the invitation to make Jesus Christ the Lord of their life. The pastor may lead them in what is often called the "sinner's" prayer.

Others may be compelled to accept Jesus as Lord and Savior as a result of hearing a message on the radio, TV, or while reading the Bible or another book (maybe even this one).

Still others are led to the Lord in a one-on-one conversation with an already-saved believer.

Repenting of your sins and believing in Jesus as the crucified and risen Savior are the first steps in becoming a believer, a follower of Jesus, a Christian. *"If you **confess** with your mouth that Jesus is Lord and **believe** in your heart that God raised him from the dead, you will be **saved**. For it is by **believing** in your heart that you are made right with God, and it is by **confessing** with your mouth that you are **saved**."* Romans 10:9-10 (NLT)

There is no strict pattern to follow in the profession of faith (sinner's prayer), yet typically it should contain some core elements. An *example* of a simple sinner's prayer that covers the key elements is as follows:

Dear God in Heaven - - - I come to you in the name of your son, Jesus - - - I admit I have sinned as all have sinned - - - I ask for Your forgiveness - - - I believe Jesus Christ shed His blood for my sins - - - and gave His life in order that I might have eternal life - - - I believe Jesus was raised from the dead by the power of Your Holy Spirit - - - Right now I accept Jesus as my Lord and Savior - - - With Your help, Jesus - - - I purpose in my heart - - - to serve You from this day forward. - - - In Jesus' name - - - Amen.

This prayer holds no weight unless the person saying it (**confessing**) is truly sorry for their sins, ready to turn away from them (**repenting**) and is committed to making Jesus the Lord of their life by acting upon their new-found faith (**believing**). A changed life is the result of true salvation! Consider this commitment carefully and do not put off the opportunity to move into a right relationship with God.

The Bible documents hundreds of promises for the believer including peace for those who accept Jesus as Lord and learn to walk according to His ways, "..... *and the peace of God, which surpasses all understanding, will guard your hearts and minds through Christ Jesus.*" Philippians 4:7 (NKJV)

God's invitation into His Kingdom extends to all of mankind. Decide to make Jesus the Lord of your life and **become the man or woman of God that He intends you to be, and that your friends and loved ones need you to be.** Once your "spiritual house is in order" and you are in a right and saved relationship with the Lord, you can play a part in helping to lead or encourage others to a saving and intimate relationship with God through Jesus Christ.

"Everyone who acknowledges me publicly here on earth, I will also acknowledge before my Father in heaven. But everyone who denies me here on earth, I will also deny before my Father in heaven." Matt. 10:32-33 (NLT)

The way you will know God's plan for your life is through a progressive, consistent and intimate relationship with God the Father, Jesus the Son and the Holy Spirit. We continue to mature as Christians as we rely upon the Holy Spirit residing within us to help us pursue and prioritize this essential relationship with God.

For your own sake as well as for all those you care about, find a church that teaches the whole counsel of God (the whole Bible) and challenges your spiritual growth and Christian walk. Search for and attend a church fellowship that believes in and yields to the power and leading of the Holy Spirit.

Avoid churches that are powerless, lukewarm, non-fruit producing, social-gospel organizations. This type of church typically does not bring a salvation message that convicts those who attend for fear of offending or losing members. In addition, they generally do not recognize or allow the move of the Holy Spirit in their congregation.

*"**Do not quench the Spirit**. Do not despise prophecies. Test all things; hold fast what is good."* 1 Thess. 5:19-21 (NKJV)

Question:
1. How can you know God's plan for your life?

Point to consider:
Attend a church where you are encouraged to mature into the effective Disciple of Christ that God desires you to be, and that your family, friends and loved ones need you to be.

CHAPTER TEN
TRINITY DISCIPLESHIP

Today the church of Jesus Christ faces opposition and circumstances different than those seen before in history. Worldwide, man has become so technology-dependent that any significant disruption to the media, smart phone, drone and internet-crazed society would have a devastating effect.

Extremist Islamic terrorism threatens every civilized country on earth as it continues its quest to establish Islam as the only religion on the planet. Beheadings, hangings, bombings, honor killings, kidnappings, torture, etc., threaten to destabilize the governmental structure of every non-Muslim nation on earth.

The global economy is teetering on the brink of implosion and the international monetary system is a facade. Communism is alive and well and blatantly trying to re-assert itself in its quest for world domination.

While these kinds of threats and challenges are relatively easy to see, there exists another threat to Christianity that many of today's believers have been reluctant to recognize and confront. This additional area of attack comes from within the Church itself.

Consider the Apostle Paul's direction to all believers to fulfill their ministry, and also a warning about the time of the great apostasy or "falling away" from the faith that is happening right now in our current generation.

"For a time is coming when people will no longer listen to right teaching. ***They will follow their own desires and will look for teachers who will tell them whatever they want to hear.*** *They will reject the truth and follow strange myths. But you should keep a clear mind in every situation. Don't be afraid of suffering for the Lord.* ***Work at bringing others to Christ. Complete the ministry God has given you."***
2 Tim. 4:3-5 (NLT) (bold added)

Evidence of the great falling away can be found in many of today's churches, pulpits, d0enominations and other so-called Christian organizations. These apostate groups have allowed false doctrine to infiltrate their teachings. They've become seduced by building their own particular "castle" and have deviated from their call to build "God's kingdom" on the truth of God's Word.

Signs of this great falling away can be seen in the rapidly escalating teaching of a repent-less social gospel and the non-existence of hell. Increasingly, many churches have realigned their focus toward well-sounding social gospel messages, but talk little about the **cross**, the **blood** of Jesus and the need of **repentance**.

Abortion is at pandemic levels throughout the world. Within today's church is the growing acceptance of gay and lesbian preachers, pastors and teachers.

Many denominations and churches have become so obsessed with building their own castle that they are reluctant to put forth any effort to assist other Christian groups outside their walls. Often in their zeal to build their own organization, a less God-dependent and a more castle-centered entity, results. The basic commands and teachings in the Bible to *"equip the saints* (believers) *to do the work of the ministry,"* Ephesians 4: 12 (NKJV) are often abandoned. Some television ministries and churches have turned into money-soliciting castles focused on growing their own financial empire.

Today many believers find themselves attending or involved with an organization, denomination or church that has slipped into the "castle building" mindset. Though they sense and want more, they aren't quite sure how to get to the more important work of building the "Kingdom of God." For many it seems easier to just let the church or organization they're a part of move forward as they stifle their own urge to press forward for all that God has for them.

In a castle-driven organization, the spiritual growth and maturing of the individual is often neglected in order to build or maintain a man-inspired castle. Encouraging an individual's intimate relationship with God through Jesus

Christ should never be sacrificed in order to build a man-designed organization or castle. This does not mean that building a congregation or denomination is not important. It just means that the building of man's castle should not supersede the building of God's Kingdom. Regardless of whether one is in a castle or kingdom-building environment, serious believers or disciples of Jesus are called to encourage, teach and disciple others.

Believers may feel inadequate about their ability to speak into the lives of others. Maybe the sin or wrong-doing of their past is a stumbling block or they believe they need a theological degree to encourage others toward Christ. Regardless of the many reasons some Christians have held back, there is something they need to know. If their motives are right and their intent is to build God's Kingdom, if they have the best interest of others at heart and use the bible as their resource, **they are duly authorized and commanded to speak God's truth.**

God expects each believer to lead and teach (disciple) others. Teach what you know and lead others to where they can be taught the truth in God's Word. Disciple, mentor, spend time with new or struggling believers, because **real disciples of Christ, disciple others!**

Believers should seek, develop and maintain what is referred to here as the **Trinity Discipleship Model**. When this structure is functioning as intended, an individual will have established an ongoing mentoring relationship with another believer (i.e. lay person, pastor, bible study leader, youth pastor, home church leader, etc.) who is **more** spiritually mature than they are. At the same time they should establish mentoring relationships with others who are **less** spiritually mature than they are and become actively involved in helping them to grow in their spiritual walk. These mentoring relationships should incorporate recurring meetings, either one-on-one or in a small group.

This is the basic structure that God has used throughout history for believers to reach the world. It is through today's committed believers that God's kingdom can grow and flourish in this age of apostasy and the great falling away.

"Though one may be overpowered by another, two can withstand him. And a threefold cord is not quickly broken." Ecclesiastes 4:12 (NKJV)

Throughout the church today, many believers have lost or possibly never had a great sense of purpose concerning their spiritual effectiveness. This condition stifles the innate search for *spiritual significance* within every man. Every believer has much to offer that could positively impact the lives of others.

When believers do not have a strong sense of spiritual purpose, they often become despondent and begin to withdraw as they feel they have little to offer. In actuality, they are being spiritually deceived. When challenged to embrace the Trinity Discipleship Model that built the kingdom of God, a paradigm shift can result.

This biblically-based sense of purpose is a component of spiritual effectiveness for believers of all ages. Developing the Trinity Discipleship Model can be of significant benefit to older believers who may be feeling inadequate or believe their season of usefulness has passed them by. Trinity discipleship helps keep those being mentored, as well as those mentoring, accountable to the plans and purposes of God.

Senior Christians can enjoy a renewed sense of spiritual purpose as they disciple others and draw from their many years of experience. Even in the secular world, the trinity method is a highly effective component of nearly every multi-level organization. The reaching of the world won't be accomplished through a great world-wide "man-controlled" religion. It will be accomplished at the grass-roots level through **Holy Spirit led revivals**, **one-on-one evangelism** and **discipleship-mentoring,** very much like the first-century church modeled.

For those who are ready to embrace their role as a spiritual mentor to others, they can start with one or two individuals or maybe a small group in an informal bible study setting. Fast food restaurants, coffee shops, workplace lunch rooms or the kitchen table in someone's home can be great places to meet.

In this crazy world with all its distractions, it is important to understand our opportunity and also our responsibility to mentor or disciple others. Castle builders enhance the growth, power and prestige of men or man-made organizations. Those who seek out mature Christian guidance in their lives, and in turn mentor others as God intends, build God's kingdom.

Questions:
1. Have you been building a man-designed "castle" or building "God's kingdom"?
2. Who is the spiritual mentor God has placed in your life to teach and encourage you in your spiritual walk?
3. Who needs you to start mentoring them?

Point to consider:
Regardless of the many reasons some Christians have held back, there is something they need to know. **If their motives are right and their intent is to build God's Kingdom, if they have the best interest of others at heart and the Bible is their resource for truth, they are duly authorized and deputized to lead others to God's truth.**

As Disciples of Christ we are commanded to walk in Christ's authority. **Real Disciples of Christ, disciple others!**

"Intentional and committed disciples of Christ, disciple others."

CHAPTER ELEVEN
YOUR STORY/HIS GLORY

"And they have defeated him because of the blood of the Lamb and because of their testimony. And they were not afraid to die." Rev. 12:11 (NLT)

The power of a Christian's testimony (the story of their salvation experience) is often unrealized or underappreciated.

Christians often repeat the powerful stories or testimonies they have heard from other Christians, and are reluctant to share their own testimony. The testimony we have heard from others is in legal terminology "hearsay." These hearsay testimonies are not stories about events that have actually happened to us directly, yet they can be helpful when speaking about the goodness of God.

There is however, something powerful about your own testimony. It is not hearsay. It's about your personal salvation experience and is more difficult for someone to refute or dismiss. It does not need to necessarily be long and over detailed. Just a bit about how things were before your salvation and what things are like now. The emphasis should be on who God is now in your life.

A personal testimony should not over stress or glamorize a pre-salvation, worldly and/or flesh-controlled lifestyle. Be careful to avoid stimulating the fleshly weakness that may still be influencing the person you are witnessing to. An exception to this is when God prompts you to share details of your past experiences.

The person you are talking to may need to feel you really understand their situation, i.e. drug or alcohol abuse, gambling addiction, adultery, illness, family violence, etc. Once they know you understand or may have experienced a similar situation to theirs, they will usually be able to start hearing what you are trying to say. When this point is reached, further reference to the old lifestyle will become less and less necessary and should be minimized moving forward.

New believers may inadvertently glamorize the old flesh-driven nature, or ramble on and "over sell" their testimony. Consider for a moment the classic, short, powerful and impossible-to-refute testimony found in the Bible about the blind man healed by Jesus.

The Pharisees were troubled by Jesus healing the blind man on the Sabbath so they inquired of the man and suggested that Jesus must be a sinner to have healed him on the Sabbath. It is at this point that the formerly blind man gave what is one of the shortest testimonies in all of recorded history. *"He answered and said, "Whether He is a sinner or not I do not know. One thing I know: that **though I was blind, now I see."*** John 9:25 (NKJV)

Many unsaved people actually long for and desire the peace and purpose they perceive in believers. When someone is "saved", unsaved people will sense in them what the Bible describes as a "peace that passes all understanding" (Phil 4:7) and will be drawn to it.

Question:

1. Describe how your new nature is obvious to others?
2. How does Romans 12:1-2 apply to your personal testimony of your salvation and life now?

Points to consider:

There is something powerful about your testimony. It is not hearsay. It's about your personal salvation experience, and like the blind man it's difficult for someone to refute or dismiss. He may not have understood everything about Jesus, but the blind man knew that Jesus changed him!

Spiritual Challenge 1: Write out the short version of your testimony.

Spiritual Challenge 2: Start praying for God to lead you to people who need to hear your testimony, and as a result may be more open to responding to God's calling on their life.

CHAPTER TWELVE
AMBASSADORS OF GOD'S LOVE

"Therefore, if anyone is in Christ, he is a new creation; old things have passed away; behold, all things have become new. Now all things are of God, who has reconciled us to Himself through Jesus Christ, and has given us the ministry of reconciliation, that is, that God was in Christ reconciling the world to Himself, not imputing their trespasses to them, and has committed to us the word of reconciliation. Now then, **we are ambassadors for Christ,** *as though God were pleading through us: we implore you on Christ's behalf, be reconciled to God. For He made Him who knew no sin to be sin for us, that we might become the righteousness of God in Him."* II Cor. 5:17-21 (NKJV)

Another profound mystery concerning God involves the love He has for us. It defies our understanding how God could love us so much that He would send His only son to die in our place and endure the penalty of our sinful nature. How could God send His Son, and how could Jesus love us to the point of obedience to the death and torture of the cross?

"For in one place the Scriptures say, "What are people that you should think of them, or a son of man that you should care for him? Yet you made them only a little lower than the angels and crowned them with glory and honor. You gave them authority over all things.

Now when it says "all things," it means nothing is left out. But we have not yet seen all things put under their authority. What we do see is Jesus, who was given a position "a little lower than the angels"; and because he suffered death for us, he is now "crowned with glory and honor." Yes, by God's grace, Jesus tasted death for everyone." Heb. 2:6-9 (NLT)

When people come to the sobering realization of what Jesus did and allow His sacrificial death to become personal to them, **something in them changes**. Jesus is no longer some historical figure that is separate and apart from that person. He becomes a living presence in that person's life as the Holy Spirit begins to indwell that person.

The presence of the Holy Spirit results in a profound sense of appreciation and thankfulness for what God has done. This begins to transform our nature. As our love for God grows and we continue to mature as Christians, the question becomes, "How do I share what Jesus has done for me with others and become an effective ambassador of God's love to the people in my life?"

In 1961, President John F. Kennedy said, *". . . Ask not what your country can do for you, ask what you can do for your country."* Though this famous quote was directed toward inspiring national patriotism, it has great significance when used to evaluate our Christian perspective.

Many people early in their lives and career have a "what's in it for me" attitude about their job, spouse, relationship with God, etc. As Christians mature a shift takes place where they change much like in the challenge of President John F. Kennedy. They become less focused on what they can get out of Christianity and more focused on what they can do to help bring the Gospel of Jesus Christ to others. The following illustration puts into perspective how our relationship with God is developed, energized and maintained.

Before the age of digital watches, luminescent material was used on watch and clock faces so you could tell what time it was in the dark. When the watch was subjected to outside light the luminescent material would absorb a certain amount of energy. When removed from the outside light source the material would expend the retained energy in the form of a visible glow. If you kept the watch away from the outside light source too long, the glow from the luminescent material on the watch would begin to weaken and eventually disappear.

This relationship between the outside light and the luminescent material on the face of the watch is a great illustration of how our spiritual influence works. When we spend time in prayer, reading the Word of God or exposing ourselves to godly teachers and leaders our spiritual energy level increases and goes with us as we venture out into the darkness of worldly influences. Believers carry with them the life-giving energy of God, as they invade the darkness with His light.

"You are the light of the world. A city that is set on a hill cannot be hidden. Nor do they light a lamp and put it under a basket, but on a lampstand, and it gives light to all who are in the house. Let your light so shine before men, that they may see your good works and glorify your Father in heaven." Matt 5:14-16 (NKJV)

If we interact with the darkness of worldly influences and do not continue to spend time with God and maintain the godly influences, our inner spiritual glow starts to weaken. We are then in danger of being influenced by the darkness, rather than influencing the darkness of the world.

In order for us to be effective ambassadors of God's love and purpose we must stay grounded in God's presence. True believers develop a lifestyle that includes daily time in prayer and worship, Bible reading, and the exclusion of ungodly and worldly influences.

The effectiveness and reach of an ambassador of Christ is extensive. A believer can intercede in prayer for anyone or anything that God brings to their mind, even though that person or situation may be on the other side of the globe. You do not need to leave your home, travel to where they are or necessarily even speak to them on the phone. You can **intercede for them in Jesus' name right where you are.**

You may never know the result of your prayer on this side of eternity. Regardless, work at and develop the daily habit of spending time in prayer for others. They, as well as you, will be blessed in your so doing.

Often in a believer's walk with the Lord, opportunities to step out in faith occur. The Holy Spirit will reveal such opportunities where God can work through you.

For most people, venturing out in public and just starting to pray with people that they do not know is difficult. It is often easier to start praying with friends or known acquaintances in less public situations. Once a believer becomes more comfortable praying for others, has gained experience and has seen God move as a result of their prayers, they will become more confident.

A quick, easy and impactful approach that believers can use to touch others with God's love is sometimes referred to as the "God's hand of favor" prayer. This can be initiated with someone you don't even know, as well as with people you do know well. I'll usually initiate it with a question,

"Do you have a quick minute?"
Given the proper conditions and available time in a situation **and especially with the prompting and presence of the Holy Spirit leading me, I then ask**, *"Have you ever heard of the expression*

'God's hand of favor?' They may be familiar with it, or if not, just add, *"It just means that God can favor whomever, or do whatever He wants to do."*

I usually add something like, *"If God's favor wasn't with David when he faced Goliath the giant, things probably wouldn't have worked out too well."*

I then say, *"I want you to think for a minute. If God's hand of favor was hovering over us right now, is there somewhere in your life that you would want Him to move His hand of favor in a positive way? You do not have to tell me what it is. It may be a financial need, a loved one's illness or a relationship issue. It doesn't matter what it is; if it matters to you God knows about it and it matters to Him."*

Give them a brief moment then ask, *"Do you have something in mind?"*

When they nod or otherwise indicate they are thinking of something, say *"Well, let's pray right now!--- Dear God in heaven, we come to you in Jesus name, the highest way we know. Now Father, I don't know what the concern is, but you do. Right now we come together in agreement and ask that your hand of favor get involved in a positive way, so much so that in days not far off that he/she would know that You've heard and answered, and because of this, his/her faith would grow even more, Amen."*

Upon praying this prayer, an immediate change often takes place. Just the fact that someone took time to pray with them about a concern they have, can be moving. The really great part is that when God answers the concern of their heart, He gets all the glory. Just stopping to pray with someone lays the groundwork for God to show Himself strong, and for that person's life to be touched by the love and power of God. "God's hand of favor" is a simple way to pray with people.

Have you ever seen someone in a wheelchair and had the urge to lay your hands on them and pray that they will regain their ability to walk? You believe in faith healing and **in your own mind's eye can actually visualize yourself** walking up to them, but you don't. You might be intimidated by others around you or you question the timing, or worry they won't get healed and you'll look foolish. You convince yourself its best you stay where you are and not take a chance on God (or you) looking bad because they didn't get healed. *Sound vaguely familiar?*

There is a pattern and method of discipleship that Jesus himself gave us in order that we can be an effective ambassador and agent for God's purposes. It is often overlooked because of the context in which it was revealed.

Without thinking about it, we are quick to dismiss what Jesus said in the following verse because we think, *'that's what Jesus did because He was the Son of God.'*

So Jesus explained, *"I tell you the truth, the Son can do nothing by himself.* ***He does only what he sees the Father doing.*** *Whatever the Father does, the Son also does."* John 5:19 (NLT)

Could we in our haste to revere Jesus, be missing the point that He was challenging us as believers to respond to the God-inspired opportunities and leading of the Holy Spirit? In Luke 10:19 Jesus gave His followers authority over evil spirits. We are to execute that authority.

In a curious sort of way, the name of one of the first personal watercraft companies provides an effective mindset that can help us to act more like Jesus in these God-ordained moments. The company was called Sea-Doo.

A slight variation of their name "See-Do" (See and do what God shows you to do) brings about a whole new meaning on how to be a more effective ambassador for Jesus Christ.

Going forward, when these God-inspired "See-Do" opportunities present themselves in your mind, be a real ambassador of God's love and do not hesitate. Get up and walk over to the guy in the wheelchair and pray for the love and the healing power of God to impact their life. If the Holy Spirit is involved as He should and needs to be, He will be waiting to partner with you there. (See the Prayer for Healing templet on page 241.)

Effective discipleship challenges:

1. Seek God's presence in prayer, read the Word of God and initiate daily praise and worship, even if it's only for 15 minutes a day to start with. This is an important step in the successful development of an intimate relationship with God.

2. Spend time daily interceding in prayer for others.

3. Seek out and be quick to respond to the "See-Do" opportunities that God creates in your life.

Points to consider:

As Christians mature a shift takes place where they change. They become less focused on what they want and more focused on what they can do to be a blessing, and to bring the gospel story to others. This command of God, to prefer others over our own self-interest, results in the love of God being demonstrated openly for all the world to see.

*"Not all doers are believers,
but all true believers are doers."*
M.C.

CHAPTER THIRTEEN
ESCAPING "LUKEWARM"

"I really like the idea of saying 'yes' to God, it's just that I'm having a little trouble saying 'no' to myself." - Miguel Charo. This is, has been and always will be the battle that wars against every believer's spiritual effectiveness.

"No temptation has overtaken you except such as is common to man; but God is faithful, who will not allow you to be tempted beyond what you are able, but with the temptation will also make a way of escape, that you may be able to bear it." 1 Corinthians 10:13 (NKJV)

This verse has led some teachers and even some pastors to incorrectly derive something that was never intended. As a result and usually with the best of intentions, they proclaim something like, *"God won't put on you more than you will be able to handle."*

If God allowed only those things that you could handle on your own, you wouldn't need Him. If what these teachers have proclaimed was true there would be no martyrs. The truth is, **God does allow** more and greater trials to come our way than we can handle. Often it is the mountain that we cannot handle that brings us to the sobering conclusion that we need God.

What this verse is really focusing on is God's faithfulness, and the way of escape that He makes available to us in **every** temptation.

Consider a man on his way home from work as he ponders the possibility of some ungodly sinful activity. It could be recklessly gambling at the casino, getting drunk with friends at the local bar, meeting up with old drug buddies and partying at one of their houses or going to meet an attractive co-worker for an adulterous affair. Also imagine this temptation that entices him lies ahead just a few miles further down the road. Yet, just two blocks ahead is the turn that leads to his home, family, godly friends or other "ways of escape."

For a fleeting moment he feels like he should force the temptation aside and make the correct godly decision. The knowing of what he should do and the wanting of what his flesh desires, are in conflict.

All of us have experienced these opportunities to avoid giving in to some type of temptation. Do we yield to the fleshly desire of the moment or look for God's way out? What we are actually experiencing in these moments is this scripture being fulfilled in our life. With every temptation God allows, He provides a way out. Yet we often don't even realize it. It is the ever present "faithfulness of God" that implores us to go the better way.

The next time you feel that God is distant, remember how close to you He must be, just to live up to this one promise in this one verse. He will meet every attempted temptation of the enemy with a way of escape. We must look for it and act decisively. Do not hesitate, for if you do you may let the way of escape slip away, and end up submitting to the sin.

Reflect back on these few paragraphs and try to become better at seeing the ways of escape God is making for you. **If you look for it, you will find it every time.**

When reading this book, the Bible, or any of the countless other books and articles on Christianity, it is fairly easy to start to see the "why" of Christianity. We understand sin and its consequences. We understand the concept of Christ's sacrifice to pay for the sin debt of mankind. We can see how God orchestrated events in the Bible to be encouraging and also other events to be warnings to mankind through the ages. Looking at things from God's perspective, we can begin to see the "why" and in many circumstances even some of the "how" of God's plan to win back and reconcile man to Himself.

As we expand our openness and willingness to pursue God and His plan for our life, the actual "how to" of our fully embracing Christianity and God's plan for us is more difficult to master.

It's not as though the truth in the Bible of us becoming all that God intends is hidden from us. Our seeming inability to reach the place of complete commitment that the Apostle Paul attained, has to do with God's plan and its diametrically opposed adversary's plan - our own individual "self-centered nature."

The foundation of becoming a modern day Paul the Apostle begins with a declaration of our *commitment* to follow and serve Christ. Paul's commitment brought him to the point that he challenged all believers in the first century and every century since to follow his example.

He made a strong declaration of his life of commitment to Christ as he approached the end of his time on earth. It is a message of encouragement and also a warning to those who would come later. He knew some would pervert the intended teachings of God toward their own selfish desires and turn away from truth.

"I charge you therefore before God and the Lord Jesus Christ, who will judge the living and the dead at His appearing and His kingdom: **Preach the word!** *Be ready in season and out of season. Convince, rebuke, exhort, with all longsuffering and teaching. For the time will come when they will not endure sound doctrine, but according to their own desires, because they have itching ears, they will heap up for themselves teachers; and they will turn their ears away from the truth, and be turned aside to fables.* **But you be watchful in all things, endure afflictions, do the work of an evangelist, fulfill your ministry.** *For I am already being poured out as a drink offering, and the time of my*

departure is at hand. I have fought the good fight, I have finished the race, I have kept the faith. Finally, there is laid up for me the crown of righteousness, which the Lord, the righteous Judge, will give to me on that Day, and not to me only but also to all who have loved His appearing." 2 Tim. 4:1-8 (NKJV)

Ask yourself, *"Am I fighting the good fight? How am I finishing the race? How well have I kept the faith?"*

I don't know about others, but when I looked at how well I'd been doing in light of Paul's example and challenge, I felt I was falling considerably short. I didn't like that feeling. I wasn't quite sure of how or what to do about it, and it got me thinking. Of course I started to try to do better but that only got me so far. My progress was being thwarted by an unseen adversary, my own self-centered nature. It was putting up a better fight than my Spirit-led nature.

Without realizing it and even though unintentionally, I had become much like the "lukewarm" group of people Jesus admonished in the Bible.

*"I know your works, that you are neither cold nor hot. I could wish you were cold or hot. So then, because you are **lukewarm**, and neither cold nor hot, I will vomit you out of My mouth."* Rev. 3:15-16 (NKJV)

It was not a very desirable condition to experience. I suspect many professing Christians may find themselves in a similar situation. Until we mature spiritually and begin to understand the enormity of the raging spiritual battle that surrounds us, there is the tendency to treat the Christian walk like a casual skirmish with the devil. We often do not adequately understand the self-centered desires within us that the devil manipulates to our detriment. He's playing for keeps in an all-out war while "lukewarm" Christians are trying to coexist with the "pet sin" they are reluctant to deal with.

Until a person comes to the realization that they are in a real "life and death war" with an enemy who is fully committed to their destruction and the destruction of everyone they care about, they are very susceptible to falling into the "lukewarm" lifestyle. **Their friends, family and loved ones are the collateral damage that will pay for their refusal to fully engage in the battle** against the forces of darkness in the spiritual realm.

For many Christians, the "lukewarm" verse in the Bible that presents a warning from Jesus is a bit troubling. Many Christians are concerned about how this might apply to them. The way to become victorious over the lukewarm nature of humanity is again found in the Bible and is patterned for all generations in what Jesus said.

"I will no longer talk much with you, for the ruler of this world (Satan) *is coming,* **and he has nothing in Me."** John 14: 30 (NKJV)

"Peace I leave with you, My peace I give to you; not as the world gives do I give to you. Let not your heart be troubled, neither let it be afraid." John 14:27 (NKJV)

The reason so many Christians are troubled by the lukewarm reference in the Bible and do not have the peace Jesus offers, is that *the ruler of this world* (Satan) still *"has something in them."*

Questions:

1. Are you walking in the peace and confidence that Jesus modeled, or is there something or some things that the ruler of this world (Satan) still has in you?

2. If so, what are you going to do about it?

Points to Consider:

When a believer totally commits to follow Jesus and rejects, renounces and repents of every worldly and sinful aspect of their life, the peace that Jesus walked in becomes alive, active and flowing in the life of that believer. The calling of Jesus is not a call to be lukewarm; it is a call to holiness.

"Pursue peace with all people, and holiness, without which no one will see the Lord." Hebrews 12:14 (NKJV)

I really like the idea of saying "YES" to God,

it's just that I'm having a little trouble

saying 'NO" to myself.

CHAPTER FOURTEEN
"KNOWING" THE LORD

So how does one go from making a profession of faith to actually transition to a lifestyle of effectively following God's plan for their life? How does one become the type of believer that others see as having a sincere faith in God; a faith that draws them toward God?

Though touched on previously, the answers are found in becoming a serious student in pursuit of God through His Word the Bible, while at the same time developing an intimate "knowing" relationship with God, through the Holy Spirit. It is just about impossible to mature into the committed disciple of Christ that God intends without doing these two things.

*"Be diligent to present yourself approved to God, a worker who does not need to be ashamed, **rightly dividing the word of truth.**"* 2 Timothy 2:15 (NKJV)

Early in their Christian walk many new believers become "spoon-fed Christians." This is actually okay in the initial stages of Christian maturing. They may make numerous contacts with a more mature believer asking things like, *"Where in the Bible does it says . . . . ?* Or ask, *"What does the Bible say about . . . . . ?"*

At some point in time, **and the sooner the better,** new believers are challenged to become a diligent student of the Bible, on their own. Their spiritual mentors and teachers will not always be immediately available. The new believer will want to be able to give the words of life (the Word of God) to the person standing right in front of them. There are no easy short cuts.

As someone diligently pursues God through His Word and in spending time in prayerful communion (conversation) with God, the reward of increased faith and belief will result. *"But without faith it is impossible to please Him, **for he who comes to God must believe that He is, and that He is a rewarder of those who diligently seek Him**."* Hebrews 11:6 (NKJV)

*"I love those who love me, **And those who seek me diligently will find me**."* Proverbs 8:17 (NKJV)

Though it comes easier for some than for others, **memorizing scripture is of great value**. New believers are encouraged to use a highlighter, write verses in a special notebook or on 3X5 cards or just underline scriptures that stand out to them in the Bible. Yes, it's okay to write in your Bible! Every now and then read the verses over and little by little memorize them. Start with just one or two, and then go on to others.

There is a section located at the back of this book containing scriptures that can be a starting place for high-lighting, underlining, etc. Reviewing the underlined or highlighted verses helps one develop a library, so to speak, of verses that can be shared with others to encourage them in their time of need.

As people become more comfortable with verses they have memorized, **they will surprisingly run across people that need to hear those same exact scriptures.** This is not a coincidence. This is God orchestrating a divine appointment and using that person to encourage someone else, and at the same time also encouraging the person who has memorized the verse.

The Bible, though it may seem a little intimidating to the new believer, is actually a wonderful friend.

"Your word is a lamp to my feet And a light to my path." Psalm 119:105 (NKJV)

"Trust in the Lord with all your heart, And lean not on your own understanding; In all your ways acknowledge Him, And He shall direct your paths." Prov. 3: 5-6 (NKJV)

There is in the Bible a compelling story that is probably one of the best examples of why it's necessary to develop an inner data bank of memorized scriptures. It is found in Matthew.

"Now when the tempter came to Him (Jesus), he said, "If You are the Son of God, command that these stones become bread." But He answered and said, "It is written, 'Man shall

not live by bread alone, but by every word that proceeds from the mouth of God."
Matthew 4:3-4 (NKJV)

When Jesus was tempted by the devil in the wilderness, He used the Word of God to resist the devil. He did not use supernatural power or call in a host of angels to defend Him. Instead He used the Word of God from the Old Testament to counter every temptation the devil set before Him. It is a pattern and templet that God modeled for us to use when we are tempted. Now, in addition to the Old Testament we have the New Testament, containing the Gospel of Jesus Christ. The books of Matthew, Mark, Luke and John record some of Jesus' own words!

In those moments when we are tempted, how can we expect the Holy Spirit to call forth those verses from within our being, unless we have put forth the effort to get them inside of us (memorized them) first? Consider what King David had to say about the importance of implanting the Word of God into his innermost being.

"Your word I have hidden in my heart, that I might not sin against You!" **Psalm 119:11 (NKJV)**

For some early in their pursuit of God, prayer may be more in the vane of praying to God "just in case He exists." For the maturing believer however, developing a strong prayer life is an essential part of becoming a true Disciple of Christ.

Prayer in your prayer closet (private place to get alone with God) is an open, one-on-one conversation with God. It is a great time to just speak with God with no one around to interfere or distract you. It's a time to listen for His response.

There are times when you pray with other believers to avail yourself of the power of believer-agreement, "in Jesus name." There are other times when you praise and worship God with others (sometimes called corporate prayer or worship). In any case, prayer is to be heart-felt, and not words mindlessly repeated over and over.

"And when you pray, do not use vain repetitions as the heathen do. For they think that they will be heard for their many words." Matthew 6:7 (NKJV)

Just talk to God like He is your closest friend, because He is. Tell God how you really feel, what is bothering you, what your hopes, dreams and concerns are, **and then wait for Him to answer**. Sometimes, you will actually "hear" Him speak words, or it may be a feeling that is difficult to fully explain. Nevertheless, it will be God revealing to you what path or course of action you should take. Too often, people rattle off their list of desires, concerns or complaints and rush off not waiting to hear what God has to say.

The Lord can speak to us through His Word or in impressions coming from the indwelling of the Holy Spirit. He can also speak to us through pastors, teachers, prophets, dreams, visions, angels and sometimes you may hear the actual audible voice of God.

Do not become solely dependent on others to intercede for you in every time of need or trouble. After all, **it is God who wants to have an intimate relationship directly with you.** He gives an open invitation to call on Him.

"Call to Me, and I will answer you, and show you great and mighty things, which you do not know." Jeremiah 33:3 (NKJV)

One of the most powerful things we can do to dramatically catapult our relationship with God to a more successful, impactful spiritual walk is to establish a set target time of alone time with God for prayer. Once established, we must maintain and guard our intimate one-on-one time with the Lord. If the cares, concerns, circumstances of life, or distractions of the enemy disrupt your alone time with God, just get back on track as soon as you can. You'll find God waiting for your return and eager to resume the journey of your life together.

Questions:

1. Who benefits from memorizing Bible verses?

2. What is your plan for memorizing Scripture?

3. Write down your plan to develop, maintain and guard your intimate one-on-one time with the Lord?

Points to consider:

God desires to have an intimate relationship with each believer. Set a target time for one-on-one prayer and Bible study, then be as diligent as possible to keep faithful to it.

"You cannot leave church on Sunday and fight a well-trained enemy all week with your pastor's sword. You have your own sword (the Word of God). Use it!"
Mike Carr Sr.

CHAPTER FIFTEEN
GOD'S BLUEPRINT – THE BIBLE

The Bible is divided into two main sections, the Old Testament and the New Testament. The books of the first part of the Bible, the Old Testament, describe the progress of God's chosen people known as Jews, Hebrews or Israelites. They were the chosen people because of a covenant God made with Abraham, the father of the Jewish nation. Though Abraham did not fully comprehend it at the time, a descendent of his would one day be born (Jesus Christ) who would save the people from their sins.

The Old Testament describes how God's chosen people did or did not serve and obey Him as they interacted with the rest of mankind. There is a recurring pattern of God's people drifting away from God and suffering the consequences, then turning back to God as they repented or turned away from their sin and rebellion.

God spoke to mankind through prophets in the Old Testament. Not only did God's prophets speak warnings regarding their ungodly behavior, they also spoke of the hope of a future Messiah. In the Hebrew language this Savior of the world was called Yeshua, and today in English, Jesus. (John 3:16) The New Testament describes the fulfillment of these prophecies.

Old Testament books provide daily wisdom and guidance for all who are willing to study them. The New Testament details the life of Jesus and gives instructions to all believers on how to follow Him and how to spread the hope of the "Good News" of Jesus' victory over death, hell and the grave.

In the Old Testament, God used a man called Moses to bring the main laws, rules or instructions for mankind to follow. The **Ten Commandments** continue to convict us of our sin and are the main moral and spiritual guidelines of godly living today. They were first recorded by Moses in the book of Exodus. The New King James Version (NKJV) of the Bible outlines them as follows:

(1) And God spoke all these words, saying: "I am the Lord your God, who brought you out of the land of Egypt, out of the house of bondage. You shall have no other gods before Me."

(2) "You shall not make for yourself a carved image, or any likeness of anything that is in heaven above, or that is in the earth beneath, or that is in the water under the earth; you shall not bow down to them nor serve them. For I, the Lord your God, am a jealous God, visiting the iniquity of the fathers on the children to the third and fourth generations of those who hate Me, but

showing mercy to thousands, to those who love Me and keep My commandments."

(3) "You shall not take the name of the Lord your God in vain, for the Lord will not hold him guiltless who takes His name in vain."

(4) "Remember the Sabbath day, to keep it holy. Six days you shall labor and do all your work, but the seventh day is the Sabbath of the Lord your God. In it you shall do no work: you, nor your son, nor your daughter, nor your male servant, nor your female servant, nor your cattle, nor your stranger who is within your gates. For in six days the Lord made the heavens and the earth, the sea, and all that is in them, and rested the seventh day. Therefore the Lord blessed the Sabbath day and hallowed it."

(5) "Honor your father and your mother, that your days may be long upon the land which the Lord your God is giving you."

(6) "You shall not murder."

(7) "You shall not commit adultery."

(8) "You shall not steal."

(9) "You shall not bear false witness against your neighbor."

(10) *"You shall not covet your neighbor's house; you shall not covet your neighbor's wife, nor his male servant, nor his female servant, nor his ox, nor his donkey, nor anything that is your neighbor's."* Exodus 20:1-17 (NKJV)

In the New Testament, Jesus gave what are sometimes referred to as the two additional "encompassing commandments."

"One of them, an expert in religious law, tried to trap him with this question: "Teacher, which is the most important commandment in the law of Moses?" Jesus replied, "'You must love the Lord your God with all your heart, all your soul, and all your mind.' This is the first and greatest commandment. A second is equally important: 'Love your neighbor as yourself.' All the other commandments and all the demands of the prophets are based on these two commandments." Mt. 22:35-40 (NLT)

Both the Old and New Testaments of the Bible are essential reading for all who seek truth and want to know who God is and how to enter into an intimate relationship with Him. God is the essence of truth.

"Jesus said to him, "I am the way, **the truth**, *and the life. No one comes to the Father except through Me."* John 14:6 (NKJV)

The 66 books of the Bible were written by inspiration of the Holy Spirit of God through a multitude of authors. The Holy Spirit is the third person of the Trinity (God the Father, God the Son - Jesus and God the Holy Spirit). This triune nature of God is another mystery that challenges man's finite understanding. They are distinctly three persons, yet they are the one true God.

The Old Testament covers approximately 4,000 years of man's history and points toward the coming of Jesus. The New Testament is the story of Jesus' birth, life, ministry, death, resurrection and prophesied second coming. It details the early beginnings of His church which began approximately 2,000 years ago.

Born of a virgin girl Mary and conceived by the Holy Spirit, Jesus was fully God and fully man. Though tempted by the devil, He did not sin as did Adam. Jesus lived a totally sinless life.

"So then, since we have a great High Priest who has entered heaven, Jesus the Son of God, let us hold firmly to what we believe. This High Priest of ours understands our weaknesses, for he faced all of the same testings we do, yet he did not sin. So let us come boldly to the throne of our gracious God. There we will receive his mercy, and we will find grace to help us when we need it most." Heb. 4:14-16 (NLT)

God promised His chosen people the Jews a redeemer for their sins. Jesus was the fulfillment of God's promise to His people as well as to all mankind. Many Jews rejected Jesus. After He ascended back to heaven, a small group of followers waited (as Jesus had previously instructed them), for the promised helper (Holy Spirit) from God the Father.

"Suddenly, there was a sound from heaven like the roaring of a mighty windstorm, and it filled the house where they were sitting. Then, what looked like flames or tongues of fire appeared and settled on each of them. And everyone present was filled with the Holy Spirit and began speaking in other languages, as the Holy Spirit gave them this ability." Acts 2:2-4 (NLT)

The Holy Spirit empowers a Christian to live according to God's Word and to be a witness of the Gospel, the "Good News" of Jesus Christ.

Jesus referred to His 12 chosen disciples as Apostles. They were joined by many converts in the first century. *"One day soon afterward Jesus went to a mountain to pray, and he prayed to God all night. At daybreak he called together all of his disciples and chose twelve of them to be apostles."* Luke 6:13 (NLT)

These men, together with many women, were responsible for spreading the Good News of

Jesus' victory over sin and death, and His incomparable love for all mankind. The message went out first to the Jews and later to the non-Jewish (Gentile) world, primarily through the missionary work of Paul the Apostle. Paul wrote many of the New Testament books of the Bible.

Questions:

1. In what ways do the Ten Commandments have relevance today?

2. What does the following bible verse mean to you?

Points to consider:

"Be diligent to present yourself approved to God, a worker who does not need to be ashamed, rightly dividing the word of truth." 2 Timothy 2:15 (NKJV)

Both the Old and New Testaments of the Bible are essential reading for all who seek truth and want to know who God is and how to enter into an intimate relationship with Him. God is the essence of truth.

CHAPTER SIXTEEN
THE TIMES AND MISSION OF JESUS

At the time of Jesus' birth the Jews lived under the rule of the Roman Empire. Throughout their history they had lived under domination by several empires, nations and kings, and by this time were desperately looking for their prophesied Messiah (deliverer/savior) to free them from their cruel Roman oppressors.

Jesus came to "destroy the works of the devil." (1 John 3:8) He was not the political Deliverer/Savior from the Romans that the Jews were looking for. He began His public ministry following His **water baptism** (immersed in water) by his cousin John the Baptist, which was followed by a 40 day period of fasting and testing by the devil. (Matthew Chapter 4)

John the Baptist was already preaching, *"Repent for the Kingdom of God is at hand."* Mt. 3:2 (NLT) This practice established water baptism as a representative act demonstrating one's repentance and dying to one's natural self-centered nature and rising out of the water as a believer who is committed to God's ways. Baptism in water continues to be an outward act of obedience to God, symbolizing the individual's allegiance to Jesus Christ.

The Jewish leaders were so focused on their religious superiority that most of them did not recognize Jesus Christ as the prophesied Messiah. In fact, the Jewish religious leaders of the day saw Jesus as a threat to their lofty positions and were largely responsible for bringing about His crucifixion and death. When the sinless Son of God was executed and subsequently rose from the dead by the power of the Holy Spirit, Satan lost the control over mankind he had gained when Adam and Eve fell (sinned) in the Garden of Eden.

Following His crucifixion Jesus broke the power of death, hell and the grave when, by the power of the Holy Spirit, He rose from the dead. Many of the hundreds of people who witnessed His return from the dead became fervent believers and began spreading the story of Jesus.

God the Father made a special declaration concerning His Son the Lord Jesus, His obedience and His name. *"He* (Christ) *made himself nothing; he took the humble position of a slave and appeared in human form. And in human form he obediently humbled himself even further by dying a criminal's death on a cross. Because of this, God raised him up to the heights of heaven and gave him a name that is above every other name, so that at the name of Jesus every knee will bow, in heaven and on earth and under the earth,* **and every tongue will confess that Jesus Christ is Lord, to the glory of God the Father.***"* Phil. 2:7-11 (NLT)

The Good News of Jesus' death and resurrection created a way for man to be reconciled with God through belief in Jesus

Christ. In the first century (as in subsequent centuries), many followers of Jesus were killed for their faith in Him. This persecution of believers continues to the present day.

Initially, the Good News of Jesus' victory spread within the Jewish community. Then at God's command, the Apostle Paul spearheaded the mission to spread the gospel of Jesus Christ throughout the non-Jewish world. He said, *For I am not ashamed of this Good News about Christ. It is the power of God at work, saving everyone who believes—the Jew first and also the Gentile (non-Jews)."* Romans 1:16 (NLT)

Subsequent to Jesus Christ's death and resurrection, all individuals who are willing to **confess sin and accept and believe** in Jesus as the risen Son of God, enters a relationship with God. Allowing the Holy Spirit to convict them of their sins results in **repentance** or the turning away from sin. In so doing, they gain the gift of eternal life. With this commitment, they are **adopted** into God's heavenly family.

In the period of Jesus' three year ministry on earth, He performed many miracles and healings that drew the people to Him. He spoke of the kingdom of God and about God's desire to establish an intimate relationship with each man. The first four books of the New Testament, Matthew, Mark, Luke and John record the main eyewitness accounts of Jesus' ministry on earth. In these Gospel books Jesus spoke about all facets of man's relationship with God and also man's responsibilities to his fellow man. These eyewitness accounts also cover Jesus' many encounters with demonic forces and the authority and the deliverance He commanded over them.

The Bible tells us that Jesus ascended bodily into heaven and that He would return again in like-manner to receive unto Himself those who believe and accept His sacrificial death and resurrection. As He ascended into heaven two angels standing among the crowd who were watching said, *"Men of Galilee, why are you standing here staring into heaven? Jesus has been taken from you into heaven, but someday he will return from heaven in the same way you saw him go!"* Acts 1:11 (NLT)

The Apostle Paul describes the future return of Jesus considered by many theologians to be an event called "the Rapture."

"We tell you this directly from the Lord: We who are still living when the Lord returns will not meet him ahead of those who have died. For the Lord Himself will come down from heaven with a commanding shout, with the voice of the archangel, and with the trumpet call of God. First, the Christians who have died will rise from their graves. Then, together with them, we who are still alive and remain on the earth will be caught up in the clouds to meet the Lord in the air. Then we will be with the Lord forever. So

encourage each other with these words." 1 Thess. 4:18(NLT)

During the last night that he spent with His apostles before His arrest and crucifixion, Jesus established the covenant and tradition of **communion.**

"Then he took a cup of wine and gave thanks to God for it. Then he said, "Take this and share it among yourselves. For I will not drink wine again until the Kingdom of God has come." He took some bread and gave thanks to God for it. Then he broke it in pieces and gave it to the disciples, saying, "This is my body, which is given for you. Do this to remember me." Luke 22:17-19 (NLT)

This doctrine of remembrance has continued on through the centuries and is practiced today when believers gather together.

Questions:
1. What is the significance of water baptism and of communion?

2. How can a person be reconciled with God?

Point to consider:

Jesus came to **"destroy the works of the devil."** (1 John 3:8) He is ready and willing to partner with you in this mission. Are you willing to partner with Him?

CHAPTER SEVENTEEN
IN ONE ACCORD?

Today there are many different Christian denominations as well as thousands of churches and other Christian groups that regularly meet together. Even though the Good News of Jesus' miraculous birth, life, death and resurrection has spread worldwide, the devil has been relentless in his undermining of the mission of Christ's church.

"Jesus came and told his disciples, "I have been given complete authority in heaven and on earth. Therefore, go and make disciples of all the nations, baptizing them in the name of the Father and the Son and the Holy Spirit. Teach these new disciples to obey all the commands I have given you. And be sure of this: I am with you always, even to the end of the age." Mt. 28:18-20 (NLT)

Many professing Christians believe their church membership or their denomination is their "ticket to heaven." Others rely on a prayer once said but never actually lived out. There are even religious factions that believe in a "Co-Redeemer" in addition to Jesus alone as Redeemer and Savior.

Some among professing Christian groups do not believe in a literal hell. They believe that everybody gets to go to heaven, even though Jesus said much about that place of eternal torment called hell. In spite of what these groups teach or would like to believe, there is no in-between place of appeal or escape after death found in the Bible. Whether someone goes to heaven does not depend on the prayers of the living said after that person dies, but rather on that person's acceptance of Jesus while they were still alive. The teaching of biblical inaccuracies gives people false hope and inadvertently the license to live more worldly than godly.

Man-inspired church doctrine or tradition does not over-rule the Word of God. The Bible clearly states,

"And just as it is destined that each person dies only once and after that comes judgment."
Heb. 9:27 (NLT)

"Yes, we are fully confident, and we would rather be away from these bodies, for then we will be at home with the Lord."
2 Cor. 5:8 (NLT)

Some denominations believe that **infant baptism** is a necessary condition of church affiliation. While water baptism is a sign of dying to self and accepting God's plan for one's life, water baptism as an infant is found nowhere in the Bible. There is however, the acceptable practice of "baby dedication" by parents, to the plan and purposes of God. This ceremony is done in many of today's churches.

The practice and doctrine of **water baptism** as outlined in the Bible is for all who are mature enough to make this important life decision. The directive for believers to be baptized can be found in Mark 16:16-18. The promise of the power to be His witness when baptized in the Holy Spirit subsequent to the salvation experience, can be found in Acts 1:8.

Baptism in water and **baptism in the Holy Spirit** as recorded in the New Testament of the Bible, are important parts of being an effective Christian influence in the lives of those around us. Jesus spoke of the **Great Commission** which is for all believers....*to go, baptize and teach others*..... and is recorded in Matthew 28:19-20. This command includes all believers.

Some denominations believe and teach that Jesus is really a glorified angel, and still some other extreme factions believe that Jesus and Satan are really brothers. The teaching of false doctrines in many denominations is extensive and needs to be countered by teaching the true and accurate Word of God.

Some Christian denominations, churches or even small groups do not teach the whole Bible, but instead skip or gloss over parts of the Bible they do not agree with or do not understand, especially in regard to the gifts and workings of the Holy Spirit. To them, the working of miracles, healings, prophecies and demonic deliverance for example, were mainly limited to the first-century Christians. Jesus gave no such limitations.

Jesus said, *"Most assuredly, I say to you, he who believes in Me, the works that I do he will do also; and greater works than these he will do, because I go to My Father. And whatever you ask in My name, that I will do, that the Father may be glorified in the Son. If you ask anything in My name, I will do it.!"* John 14:12-14 (NKJV)

Jesus instructed His disciples to wait on the Holy Spirit to come to them before they set out on their mission to spread the Good News of His victory over sin and death.

"And now I will send the Holy Spirit, just as my Father promised. But stay here in the city until the Holy Spirit comes and fills you with power from heaven." Luke 24:49 (NLT)

Accepting Jesus Christ as one's personal Savior results in the initial partnering so-to-speak between God's Holy Spirit and the spirit of that person. There is an available subsequent **filling** with the Holy Spirit (often referred to as the **baptism in the Holy Spirit**) found in Acts 1:8 that can occur in a believer's life. This makes additional power and gifts available to that believer.

Jesus said, *"If you love me, obey my commandments. And I will ask the Father, and he will give you another Advocate, who will never leave you. He is the Holy Spirit, who leads into all truth. The world cannot receive him, because it isn't looking for him and doesn't recognize him. But you know him,* **because he lives with** *you now and later will be in you."* John 14:15-17 (NLT)

"I am telling you these things now while I am still with you. But when the Father sends the Advocate as my representative—that is, the Holy Spirit—he will teach you everything and will remind you of everything I have told you." John 14:25-26 (NLT)

Questions:

1. Is the church more effective operating within its own man-designed denominational traditions, or more effective "partnering" with the Holy Spirit?

2. What are some of the benefits to the individual believer of "partnering" with the Holy Spirit?

Point to consider:

In prayer, ask God if the baptism in His Holy Spirit is part of His plan to use you to reach others in these days of turmoil; then wait for Him to answer.

"Call to Me, and I will answer you, and show you great and mighty things, which you do not know. Jeremiah 33:3 (NKJV)

CHAPTER EIGHTEEN
THE PERSON OF THE HOLY SPIRIT
(Who is the Holy Spirit?)

He is the third person of the Trinity.

He is the Spirit of God who "hovered over the waters" awaiting the Word to create the world. (Genesis 1:2)

He is the Spirit of God who came upon the Virgin Mary, and she conceived Jesus. (Mt. 1:20, Luke 1:35)

He is the Spirit of God who was present (dove-symbol) and part of Jesus' baptism in the Jordan River. (Mt. 3:16-17)

He is the Spirit of God who drove Jesus into the wilderness for His time of testing with the devil. (Mt.4:1)

And most significantly, He is the Spirit and the power of God who raised Jesus from the dead and lives in all disciples of truth.

"The Spirit of God, who raised Jesus from the dead, lives in you. And just as he raised Christ from the dead, he will give life to your mortal body by this same Spirit living within you." Romans 8:11 (NLT)

According to the book of Acts, on the day of Pentecost 120 of Jesus' followers were gathered and awaiting the promised gift of God the Father. A sound as a "rushing mighty wind" filled the room (a manifestation of the presence of the Holy Spirit). The Holy Spirit filled Jesus' followers as *"divided tongues as of fire"* appeared upon each one.   Acts 2:3 (NKJV)

Together, these 120 believers worshipped God as they spoke in other "tongues" (a special God-given prayer language). They were filled with power and boldness to be witnesses of the Good News of Jesus Christ.

The Holy Spirit continues to work God's purposes, daily reminding the believer of Jesus, His teachings and His character. This same Spirit of God is at work in today's believers who display sincere faith in Jesus Christ.

The Holy Spirit represents Jesus and functions as a Comforter, Teacher, Counselor, Protector, Provider, Deliverer and Healer, to name a few. Mankind is able to have an encounter with God because of the Holy Spirit. He reveals God's love, will and plans to believers.

A major work of the Holy Spirit is to convict the sinner of sin. Sometimes he speaks to us in our own mind's "self-talk" voice that is always playing. Other times, He may convict us through a feeling that what we have done, what we are doing or what we are thinking about doing, is either right or wrong. Regardless, the

Holy Spirit will use whatever mechanism or tool necessary to make us aware of our sinful nature.

This conviction of sin by the Holy Spirit is done to help bring us to the point of understanding our need of salvation, and the need for us to repent and accept Jesus as Lord and Savior. This is the beginning stage of a right relationship with God.

Holy Spirit conviction is not our enemy, but rather one of our greatest allies and a demonstration of God's ongoing love for us. Sometimes people misunderstand the conviction of, the correction of, or the chastening of the Lord. But in reality, it is actually God's love for us that triggers the conviction of the Holy Spirit in our lives.

"My son, do not despise the chastening of the Lord, Nor detest His correction; For whom the Lord loves He corrects, Just as a father the son in whom he delights." Prov. 3:11-12 (NKJV)

Another major work of the Holy Spirit is to pour God's love into the hearts of people so that they begin to love God and love one another.

"A new commandment I give to you, that you love one another; as I have loved you, that you also love one another. By this all will know that you are My disciples, if ye have love for one another." John 13:34-35 (NKJV)

Some denominations exclude the Holy Spirit from the Godhead teaching a dual Godhead as Father and Son only. Beware of those who discredit and dishonor the third person of the Trinity.

Today many denominations limit the person of Holy Spirit and teach that many workings of the Holy Spirit have ceased. They do not believe the gifts of the Holy Spirit such as miraculous healings, speaking in tongues and prophecy occurs in the present day.

As a result, some believers settle for operating in their own boldness, rather than the more effective *"baptized in the Holy Spirt"* **power that is available to all believers**. This does not mean that they are not "saved", only that they have not as yet and may never in this life, ask for and receive the full power of the baptism in the Holy Spirit.

Throughout history there have been believers who did not experience being "baptized" in the Holy Spirit with the evidence of speaking in other tongues, but did accomplish much for the kingdom of God. They certainly will not be excluded from heaven because they never spoke in tongues while living here on earth. According to the bible, they will be rewarded for their faithful response to His Word. (Mt. 5:12, 16:27; I Cor. 3:8; Ps. 19:8, 11)

Jesus proclaimed why He came to earth: *"The Spirit of the Lord is upon Me, Because He has anointed Me To preach the gospel to the poor; He has sent Me to heal the brokenhearted, To proclaim liberty to the captives And recovery of sight to the blind, To set at liberty those who are oppressed; To proclaim the acceptable year of the Lord."* Luke 4:18-19 (NKJV)

In the writings of John the Apostle we find a rather direct and more targeted description of Jesus' mission on earth. *" . . . . . . But the Son of God (Jesus)* ***came to destroy these works of the devil.****"* 1 John 3:8 (NLT)

In the book of Matthew Jesus commanded His disciples and like-wise all believers to, *"Heal the sick, cleanse the lepers, raise the dead, cast out demons."* Mt. 10:8 (NKJV)

It is very difficult to fulfill Jesus' commandments without fully partnering with the Holy Spirit of God and being "baptized" in His power.

"I am the vine, you are the branches. He who abides in Me, and I in him, bears much fruit; ***for without Me you can do nothing.****"* John 15:5 (NKJV)

In addition to the special gifts of the Holy Spirit, the Bible lists some of the resulting benefits and traits (fruits of the Spirit) found in the life of a believer.

"But the Holy Spirit produces this kind of fruit in our lives; **love, joy, peace, patience, kindness, goodness, faithfulness, gentleness and self-control.** *There is no law against these things!"* Gal. 5: 22-23 (NLT)

Rightly respecting the Holy Spirit of the Trinity is of paramount importance and can be easily misunderstood if incorrectly taught. It is so significant that the blasphemy against Holy Spirit can result in what is often called **the unpardonable sin.** This sin has been extensively debated amongst Bible scholars.

The term "blasphemy" is associated with profanity, sacrilege, wickedness, violation and desecration when attributed to God. Some schools of thought define blasphemy as speaking against the righteous nature and person of God, or attributing the workings of God to the devil or some other non-God entity. Regardless of the multifaceted aspects of blasphemy, the Bible gives special warnings about speaking against the third person of the Trinity, Holy Spirit.

The Bible instructs us, *"And do not bring sorrow to God's Holy Spirit by the way you live. Remember, he is the one who has identified you as his own, guaranteeing that you will be saved on the day of redemption."* Ephesians 4:30 (NLT)

"I assure you that any sin can be forgiven, including blasphemy; **but anyone who**

blasphemes against the Holy Spirit will never be forgiven. It is an eternal sin." Mk 3:28-29 (NKJV)

Doing things that are displeasing to God, or not doing the things that God would have us do, grieves the Holy Spirit. Actually speaking against the Holy Spirit or against the workings of Holy Spirit can result in grave consequences. We should be very careful when it comes to what we say or do concerning this sacred trust.

"For it is impossible to bring back to repentance those who were once enlightened— those who have experienced the good things of heaven and shared in the Holy Spirit, who have tasted the goodness of the word of God and the power of the age to come— and who then turn away from God. It is impossible to bring such people back to repentance; by rejecting the Son of God, they themselves are nailing him to the cross once again and holding him up to public shame." Heb. 6:4-6 (NLT)

Some denominations are adamant in their teaching against the modern-era workings of the Holy Spirit. They often reference I Corinthians 13:8 (NKJV) *". . . Love never fails. But whether there are prophecies, they will fail; whether there are tongues, they will cease; whether there is knowledge, it will vanish away."*

They believe these workings of Holy Spirit ended with the first century apostles and that the practice and teaching of modern-day baptisms in the Holy Spirit and the associated miraculous workings of Holy Spirit, are in error.

A full reading of I Corinthians 13: 6-10 in the New Living Translation of the Bible makes it clear that these workings of Holy Spirit would no longer be needed once Jesus returned (***the perfect comes***) at the end of the age. It is in no way meant or inferred that Holy Spirit would cease His special works and gifts when the apostles died.

"Love will last forever, but prophecy and speaking in unknown languages and special knowledge will all disappear. Now we know only a little, and even the gift of prophecy reveals little! But when the end comes, these special gifts will all disappear." I Cor. 13:8-10 (NLT)

These New Testament verses were written **after** Jesus had already risen from the dead and ascended back to heaven. At the same time, they were written over two thousand years **before** the prophesied end comes. Once Jesus returns and sets everything in right order there will be no need to prophesy or for miraculous healings.

A question for those who believe that miraculous healings have ceased is, "How do you explain all the miraculous healings that occurred after the end of the first century?" These events include recent occurrences, as well as countless healings recorded over the centuries. Doctors and scientists in many of these cases testify to the miraculous nature of these healings and the absence of medicine or science.

Question:

1. As you contemplate the power of Holy Spirit and the denominational differences that exist, why not ask God to reveal His truth about His Holy Spirit directly to you, and then wait for His answer?

2. Write down what truth was revealed to you by God.

Points to Consider:

Holy Spirit' conviction is not our enemy, but rather one of our greatest allies and a demonstration of God's ongoing love for us. A major work of Holy Spirit is to pour His love into the hearts of people so that they begin to love God and love one another.

CHAPTER NINETEEN
DON'T STOP HIM!

Holy Spirit is God's gift to mankind and He emboldens and empowers the believer.

*"So if you sinful people know how to give good **gifts** to your children, how much more will your heavenly Father **give the Holy Spirit** to those who ask Him?"* Luke 11:13 (NLT)

A clear example of the saved-believer compared to the "baptized in the Holy Spirit believer," is found in the Biblical story of Holy Spirit's visitation with Jesus' disciples.

"On the day of Pentecost all the believers were meeting together in one place. Suddenly, there was a sound from heaven like the roaring of a mighty windstorm, and it filled the house where they were sitting. Then, what looked like flames or tongues of fire appeared and settled on each of them. And everyone present was filled with the Holy Spirit and began speaking in other languages, as the Holy Spirit gave them this ability." Acts 2:1-4 (NLT)

In this scripture we see believers gathered together (already **partnered** with Holy Spirit in their belief in Christ), and then we see their **empowered and gifted state** after Holy Spirit "fully baptized them." It is interesting to note that immediately after the "baptism in the Holy Spirit" visitation, something miraculous happened. Peter who was once reluctant to speak up for Jesus went out and spoke boldly, resulting in 3,000 souls being saved and won to the Lord Jesus Christ in one day!

"Then Peter continued preaching for a long time, strongly urging all his listeners, "Save yourselves from this crooked generation!" Those who believed what Peter said were baptized and added to the church that day—about 3,000 in all." Acts 2:40-41 (NLT)

God has made **great transformational gifts** available to all mankind, one being the gift of **salvation**, *"God saved you by his special favor when you believed. And you can't take credit for this; it is a gift from God. Salvation is not a reward for the good things we have done, so none of us can boast about it."* Eph. 2: 8-9 (NLT)

The Apostle Peter further affirmed the transformational **gift of the baptism in the Holy Spirit** to believers.

"Each of you must repent of your sins, turn to God, and be baptized in the name of Jesus Christ to show that you have received forgiveness for your sins. **Then you will receive the gift of the Holy Spirit. This promise is to you, and to your children, and even to the Gentiles** *—all*

who have been called by the Lord our God." Acts 2:38-39 (NLT)

"If you then, being evil, know how to give good gifts to your children, how much more will your heavenly Father give the Holy Spirit to those who ask Him!" Luke 11:13 (NKJV)

Again, subsequent to the gift of the salvation experience, gifts of the Holy Spirit are also available to **all** believers.

*"There are different kinds of spiritual gifts, but the same Spirit is the source of them all. There are different kinds of service, but we serve the same Lord. God works in different ways, but it is the same God who does the work in all of us. A spiritual gift is given to each of us so we can help each other. To one person the Spirit gives the ability to give **wise advice**; to another the same Spirit gives a message of **special knowledge**. The same Spirit gives **great faith** to another, and to someone else the one Spirit gives the gift of **healing**. He gives one person the power to **perform miracles**, and another the ability to **prophesy**. He gives someone else the ability to **discern whether a message is from the Spirit of God or from another spirit**. Still another person is given the ability to **speak in unknown languages**, while another is given the ability to **interpret** what is being said. It is the one and only*

Spirit who distributes all these gifts. He alone decides which gift each person should have." 1 Cor. 12:4-11 (NLT)

It is clear in these scriptures that Holy Spirit is an available, active, and powerful presence in the life of all believers. As the end-times approach there is a dramatic increase in the manifestation of prophecy world-wide among believers yielding to this gift and to the leading of Holy Spirit.

Quite often Holy Spirt speaks using the **prophetic gift** of a person to encourage others to boldly move forward in whatever particular gifting that the Holy Spirit has for them. The Holy Spirit also speaks through those yielded to the prophetic gift to get the attention of non-believers, that they might become receptive to the reality, the supernatural power and love of God.

Christian denominations can differ in the path to salvation and the spiritual gifts available to believers. These divisions often make non-believers reluctant to seriously consider the pursuit of God through Christianity. They fear choosing the wrong denomination or wrong church family.

This perceived confusion and dis-unity of the modern Christian church is an unfortunate stumbling block to non-believers. It is however, an effective tool the devil continues to use to keep people from intimately knowing Jesus.

Denominational competition results in a lack of effectiveness within the body of Christ. Jesus addressed this when his disciples reported individuals who were operating in His name, but were not part of the intimate inner circle of Jesus' twelve disciples. His warning still holds true for His church to the present day.

John said to Jesus, *"Teacher, we saw someone using your name to cast out demons, but we told him to stop because he wasn't in our group." "**Don't stop him!**" Jesus said. "No one who performs a miracle in my name will soon be able to speak evil of me.* ***Anyone who is not against us is for us.****"* Mark 9:38-40 (NLT)

Tragically, many of today's churches are inadvertently producing members who are busy in the ministry or with some aspect of serving in the church, but who lack in their diligent pursuit of an **intimate relationship** with God. Some believe their church or denomination association, or some denominational-inspired ritual or ceremony is their "ticket to heaven." Busy as they may be, and regardless of the considerable "good works" they might do, they might miss God's plan for their life because they did not develop an **intimate** relationship with the Lord while on earth.

"On judgment day many will tell me, 'Lord, Lord, we prophesied in your name and cast out demons in your name and performed many

*miracles in your name.' But I will reply, **'I never knew you**. Go away; the things you did were unauthorized.'"* Mt. 7:22-23 (NLT)

Traits found in the committed Christian include a sense of **reverence** for the Word of God, a **hunger** to be like Jesus (the living Word of God) and a genuine **yielding** to the leading of the Holy Spirit. This results in love for God, repentance from sin, and a **sincere effort** to love others in order to help bring them to an intimate relationship with the Lord Jesus Christ.

Questions:

1. Which of the gifts and workings of the Holy Spirit or God are still available to the modern day believer? Why?

2. Describe how a church body should function concerning spiritual gifts, as outlined in 1 Corinthians 12: 4-11.

Points to consider:

Holy Spirit is *the One who comes alongside* and is ready to partner with you in the battle that lies ahead in your life. He is the mighty power of God made available to each believer. By faith, you have to step into the battle of your own accord, and partner with Him.

CHAPTER TWENTY
SIGNS OF THE TIMES

History teaches us that a recurring pattern of the moral decline of a civilization has proven itself to be a precursor to the complete social decline and ruin of that civilization.

A few compelling examples of moral decline today include the rapid growth in pornography, human sex trafficking, the persistent onslaught from gay and lesbian groups to force the acceptance of their lifestyle in all facets of society and the current attack on the sanctity of marriage between one man and one woman.

Often when people are confronted with seemingly overwhelming situations they may easily start to think that suicide might be the "only way out." This has led to a dramatic escalation in the rate of suicide, especially in the youth and young adult population.

While modern science and social awareness of mental illness related issues concerning suicide changes, the spiritual component of these kinds of teachings need to be infused with the truth of God's ability and desire to see them through this difficult time.

Consider these spiritual truths. God cannot give a person "bad advice" or direct them to do something harmful to themselves. That would be against His character and nature. If God decided it was time for someone to die, He does not need their help. He could just "turn off" the life force of that person.

The other truth is that Satan cannot give a person "good advice." That would be against his destructive character and nature. When it comes to determining where the voice from the spiritual realm encouraging suicide comes from, there is only one answer. They are not coming from God.

If committing suicide would result in someone transitioning right to heaven, Satan because of his destructive nature, could not encourage someone to commit such an act.

What is the difference between taking the life of someone who is making a person's life difficult and they don't like the way things are going, and taking their own life because they don't like the way things are going? The problem in either case is that both involve taking life that is sacred unto God. Taking a life that is sacred unto God and then having to stand before Him and account for that action is a place no one would ever want to find themselves.

If you suspect that someone needs to know the true nature, source and intention of spiritually motivated "suicide thoughts," or that they need to know these truths to share with others they come across in life, **tell them the truth about God's desire to see them through their difficult circumstances.** Sharing these things just might help keep them from making one of the worst mistakes they could make.

The world-wide acceptance of abortion as an answer to inconvenient pregnancy or as a means of population control is further evidence of civilization's pandemic moral decline. Proponents of this and many other ungodly perspectives believe that an all-loving God accepts these behaviors when in reality they are deceiving only themselves.

It is true that Jesus' sacrifice was a full and complete payment for all of the sins committed by mankind. However, believers **must demonstrate faith by declaring and accepting Jesus' redemptive and sacrificial work by repenting of sin and standing for truth as presented in God's Word.** This transformation forms the foundation of our salvation experience and results in our diligently serving Him.

Enacting laws and instituting policies as a nation does not change God's Word nor does it convince Him to be more permissive. **God loves and has already forgiven** the drunkard, and will accept him into heaven if he **repents and forsakes** his lifestyle of sin. **God loves and has already forgiven** the adulterer, and will accept him into heaven if he **repents and forsakes** his lifestyle of sin. **God loves and has already forgiven** the lesbian and homosexual, and will accept them into heaven if they **repent and forsake** their lifestyle of sin.

God loves and has already forgiven all sinners. He will accept them into heaven if they

repent and forsake their lifestyle of sin **and accept Jesus' sacrifice for their salvation.**

God has made a way through Jesus for all people to be forgiven and gain access to heaven. Since the Bible makes it clear *". . . all have sinned and fallen short of the glory of God."* (Romans 3:23 NKJV), it's up to everyone to believe in Jesus' sacrifice for their sin, **repent** (turn away from their sin) and accept His forgiveness. Jesus said, *"No, and I tell you again that **unless you repent, you will perish, too.**"* Luke 13:5 (NLT)

Even though Jesus paid for the sins of all mankind, it is clear from Jesus' words that people whose sins have been paid for **could miss heaven if they refuse to repent and turn away from their sin.**

"Don't you realize that those who do wrong will not inherit the Kingdom of God? Don't fool yourselves. Those who indulge in sexual sin, or who worship idols, or commit adultery, or are male prostitutes, or practice homosexuality, or are thieves, or greedy people, or drunkards, or are abusive, or cheat people— ***none of these will inherit the Kingdom of God. Some of you were once like that. But you were cleansed;*** *you were made holy; you were made right with God by calling on the name of the Lord Jesus Christ and by the Spirit of our God."* 1 Cor. 6:9-11 (NLT)

In cases where someone experiences a non-typical slip into sin and then repents and turns back to God, there is restoration. God commands us to go after those enticed by sin in an attempt to bring them back from the path of destruction they are following.

"Dear brothers and sisters, if another believer is overcome by some sin, you who are godly should gently and humbly help that person back onto the right path. And be careful not to fall into the same temptation yourself." Gal. 6:1 (NLT)

Those who **habitually practice** the behaviors listed in these verses and refuse to repent and turn away from their sin, **will not gain heaven**. Instead, they will suffer in eternal torment and be separated from God just like Satan and his fallen angel followers.

Some people may be in an adulterous affair or living together as an unmarried couple, or engaged in unmarried sexual activities. Others may be controlled by drugs or involved in a gay or lesbian lifestyle. Still others may be involved in any of the situations that the Bible so strongly warns against in these verses. **The role of Christians is to love them into the family of God by sharing God's love in word and deed. Condemning them, or otherwise acting in a hurtful negative way, is against the love Jesus commanded believers to exemplify.**

Warning those caught in these specific behaviors, **in as loving a way as possible,** is the mandate of every true believer. Ignoring, overlooking, or otherwise failing to challenge these costly behaviors may seem much easier and less risky, however a Christian who really "loves others" cannot remain silent.

It is also important to understand the sometimes controversial, true role of angels in the Bible. They are described as "ministering spirits."

"But to which of the angels has He ever said: "Sit at My right hand, Till I make Your enemies Your footstool? Are they not all ministering spirits sent forth to minister for those who will inherit salvation?" Heb. 1:13-14 (NKJV)

"Do not forget to entertain strangers, for by so doing some have unwittingly entertained angels," Hebrews 13:2 (NKJV)

More so than most people realize, angels are at work in our lives. They are often seen in visions and dreams as well as actually playing part in the everyday flow of our earthly existence. Often we do not perceive them as being angels until later when we reflect on the visitation and the circumstances involved, we may come to the conclusion, *"That must have been an angel!"*

There are "good" ministering angels submitted to and operating according to God's plan and purposes and there are "bad" angels submitted to and operating according to Satan's plan and purposes.

There are three different groups of angels mentioned in the Bible, "cherubim, seraphim and archangels." The Hebrew bible clearly mentions three main angels in Scripture by name, the archangels Michael, Gabriel and Lucifer (considered originally as an archangel).

Michael the archangel could be described as the administrative enforcer of the angelic spiritual realm. In the Old Testament, Michael contended with Satan (Lucifer) over the body of Moses. Much later in the book of Revelation, we see Michael acting as a minister of God's judgment when he, at God's command, casts Satan into the bottomless pit for 1,000 years.

The second named archangel is Gabriel, God's messenger. In his own words in Luke 1:19 Gabriel answered Zacharias, *"I am Gabriel, who stands in the presence of God, and was sent to speak to you and bring you these glad tidings."* Gabriel was also the messenger of God who brought the joyous news of Jesus' coming birth to Mary, who would soon be the mother of Jesus.

The third angel named in Scripture (considered originally as an archangel) is Lucifer or Satan. In the numerous references to the main adversary of God and of mankind, of particular note is God's warning in II Corinthians 11: 13-14 about Satan's ability to deceive man and to be transformed into an "angel of light."

Some theologians believe and teach a difference between demons and fallen angels. They believe fallen angels are more powerful and have abilities beyond demons. Engaging in spiritual confrontation with demons or fallen angels should only be done with mature Christians who are well-experienced in this area.

Another sign of the times are the ever-increasing reports of angelic visitations. Certainly many of these are legitimate God-ordained events, however these visitations are never to lead to an out-of-order angel obsession or angel worship. In increasing regularity, angels are being sensationalized and glorified in television and movies.

Many of today's youth can tell you little about the Word of God, but they can go into great detail about the fictionalized angel characters depicted in science-fiction books, television series and horror films. *"... Such things ought not be so."* James 3:10 (NKJV)

Questions:
1. What does habitual sin mean?
2. What do you believe about angels?

Point to consider:
If you slipped into sin or behavior that could end up costing you heaven, would you hope that God would send someone to help bring you back from the brink of destruction?

CHAPTER TWENTY ONE
THE DECEPTION OF COMPROMISE

A very successful strategy of our enemy, the devil, is to slowly erode the Christian moral character of an individual, an organization or a nation. The devil does this by telling us lies about the truth of God.

Throughout human history this has been accomplished using a process that is sometimes referred to as "incrementalism." This simply means to slowly move toward achieving a goal a little bit at a time.

In terms of the spiritual attack on the body of believers in Jesus Christ, the enemy uses the incremental strategy to effect what has been called the "deception of compromise." This targets a weakness within the modern Church.

In every area of today's society whether entertainment, social media, politics, education, government, family, sexual orientation or the church itself, there is a **growing pressure to compromise** with worldliness and ungodliness. Because parents, teachers, leaders and governments do not want to be perceived as **intolerant**, they **little by little** give in to these incremental advances by the enemy.

This strategy is often unknowingly advanced when family members for example, watch programming, attend events and/or engage in activities that systematically and morally desensitize children, teens and even adults. In the church it can manifest itself in the form of initiating programs and events that are intended to make the church look more attractive, by attempting to look a little more like the world.

A church desiring to appeal to the general public can unknowingly circumvent God's purpose and plan. Quite often, these well-intended "worldly-appearing" plans, events and programs result in the same kind of problems that occur in similar secular world activities. The desired goal of moving people toward a more spiritual, Christ-centered lifestyle is unintentionally missed.

In American society this deception can manifest itself in the media, church pulpits and also in the legislative and judicial arenas. Again, compromise and silence takes on the form of yielding to and allowing the advance of ungodly principles. Examples of this include but are not limited to, the acceptance and protection of abortion, gay marriage, pornography, and the removal of Christian influence from schools and many other facets of society. Systematically, God and Christian references to God are being taken out of our schools, the workplace, the media and from all forms of public display. It has become illegal to post the Ten Commandments in many public places.

Why have many parents, pastors, community leaders, politicians and adults in general, neglected to stand up against the ungodly influences attacking the church and other moral principles throughout society? Is it for fear of being perceived as out-of-touch, intolerant, hypocritical, not being politically-correct or in the case of politicians, fear of becoming un-electable?

An easy way to see the dramatic escalation of the assault on Christian values is to look at the shift in the perceived reported public opinion in the last few decades. Since the horrific U.S. Supreme Court decision of 1973, the practice of abortion has become so accepted by the mainstream population that to date an estimated over 60 million babies have been "legally" murdered. The 1973 U.S. Supreme Court justices acting against the intent of nearly 200 years of prior legal rulings, created this abomination.

For centuries, the practice of homosexual activities has been looked down upon and in many cultures is still considered a crime. Today, homosexuality (the gay and lesbian agenda) has made great progress in demanding acceptance and "rights" in the United States. The increasing introduction of gay and lesbian characters, plots and subplots in movies, sit-coms, action adventure films, books, etc., has helped foster the idea that homosexuality is acceptable and just a "normal" function of sexuality.

Even though the United States was firmly founded on biblical principles, those with anti-Christian intentions have successfully usurped

Christian holidays, public events and policies, local and national laws, the entire educational system and even Christian prayer in public. Unfortunately, they have made considerable progress in undermining almost every vestige of America's Christian heritage.

In the Bible, Jesus addressed the danger of allowing a little "leaven or yeast" which represents sin, wrongdoing and the wrong teaching of the leaders of His day, to spoil God's purpose and plan.

Then Jesus said unto them, *"Why can't you understand that I'm not talking about bread? So again I say, 'Beware of the yeast of the Pharisees and Sadducees."* The yeast refers to the wrong teaching of the Jewish religious leaders in Jesus' time as recorded in Matthew 16:11-12 (NLT).

The enemy will gladly take every bit of ground Christians allow him to take. Our children and all future generations will pay for our compromise. It is time for the disciples of truth to stand up against the "deception of compromise" of the enemy. It's time to close the open gates the enemy has had access to in our lives, our families, businesses, churches, government and our society in general.

Jesus spoke of His motive and the motive of the thief, His adversary the devil.

"The thief's purpose is to steal and kill and destroy. My purpose is to give them a rich and satisfying life." John 10:10 (NLT)

Homosexuality, extra-marital affairs and those involved in sex outside of marriage are examples of individuals and society yielding to the deception of the devil for the sake of convenience or "rights." Even though it may appear easier to compromise with the subtle deception of the devil in the moment, the Bible instructs us clearly not to do so.

*"You adulterers! Don't you realize that friendship with this world makes you an enemy of God? I say it again, that **if your aim is to enjoy this world, you can't be a friend of God.**"* James 4:4 (NLT)

"And everyone will hate you because you are my followers. But the one who endures to the end will be saved." Mark 13:13 (NLT)

There is no compromise with the devil that does not result in greater loss in the end. In the United States, speaking out firmly against these immoral and biblically-condemned behaviors is viewed as intolerant and is beginning to be considered as "hate crimes." Nevertheless, it's time for the church to firmly and unabashedly speak up and say "NO" to all destructive, subtle attacks of compromise.

Questions:

1. In what areas have you contributed to or allowed the deception of compromise to erode your spiritual beliefs and effectiveness?

2. How does a Disciple of Truth, a believer in Jesus Christ, combat the "deception of compromise" that is eroding the moral foundation of our society?

Points to consider:

In terms of the spiritual attack on the body of believers in Jesus Christ, the enemy uses the incremental strategy to effect what has been called the "deception of compromise." This targets a weakness within the modern Church.

The enemy will gladly take every bit of ground Christians allow him to take. Our children and all future generations will pay for our compromise.

CHAPTER TWENTY TWO
ENEMY STRONGHOLDS

Spiritual strongholds can be anything that dominates us, separates us from God or controls us more than the purposes of God. Many new believers have difficulty in recognizing areas in which the devil is especially effective in sabotaging their Christian walk. Mature Christians can also struggle with strongholds of sin in their lives.

Although there are many types of strongholds, there are three areas that maturing Christians must learn to deal with. They are **tithing, un-forgiveness and pride.**

An old expression in the church is, *"baby Christians cut their teeth on tithing."* Money is a powerful influence in our lives. Many believers do not give God the ten percent of their increase or income (tithing), as directed in the Bible. They fail to understand that God does not need their money. God has instituted the "tithe" as a way for us to be able to partner with Him in His plan and purpose on earth. It is also a means of testing and maturing Christians.

As Christians begin to tithe and have more faith in God than in their money, God will bless them beyond what they could ever have accomplished with 100% of their income. If Satan can keep believers trusting more in their money than in God, he in effect robs them of the blessings God has for them.

In the book of Malachi, God gives a strong message of blessings and also a warning concerning tithing.

"Should people cheat God? Yet you have cheated me! "But you ask, 'What do you mean? When did we ever cheat you?' "You have cheated me of the tithes and offerings due to me. You are under a curse, for your whole nation has been cheating me. Bring all the tithes into the storehouse so there will be enough food in my Temple. If you do," says the LORD of Heaven's Armies, "I will open the windows of heaven for you. I will pour out a blessing so great you won't have enough room to take it in! Try it! **Put me to the test!** *Your crops will be abundant, for I will guard them from insects and disease. Your grapes will not fall from the vine before they are ripe," says the LORD of Heaven's Armies. "Then all nations will call you blessed, for your land will be such a delight," says the LORD of Heaven's Armies."* Mal. 3:8-12 (NLT)

Another major stronghold that undermines Christian effectiveness is in the area of **unforgiveness**. Many Christians are sabotaging their spiritual effectiveness and are actually risking their eternal salvation by harboring unforgiveness.

When one refuses to forgive someone for a transgression against them, there is often very little pain or consequence experienced by the offending party. It is the one refusing to forgive that is consumed with the bitterness that unforgiveness brings. Jesus warned there is great risk inherent in unforgiveness.

"If you forgive those who sin against you, your heavenly Father will forgive you. ***But if you refuse to forgive others, your Father will not forgive your sins."*** Mt. 6:14-15 (NLT)

Pride is probably the most predominant stronghold in the enemy's arsenal. It is after all, the transgression that cost Satan his heavenly position and is a large part of his attack on mankind. Pride is inherent in all sin. Some form of it is present in our rebellion, our greed, our lust, our unforgiveness, etc.

"Do not love this world nor the things it offers you, for when you love the world, you do not have the love of the Father in you. For the world offers only a craving for physical pleasure, a craving for everything we see, and pride in our achievements and possessions. These are not from the Father, but are from this world. And this world is fading away, along with everything that people crave. But anyone who does what pleases God will live forever." 1 John 2:15-17 (NLT)

These three strongholds are not the only strongholds that undermine man's spiritual effectiveness. Some of the more obvious strongholds are excessive drinking or gambling, illegal drug use, pornography, homosexuality or other sex-related obsessions. In the Old Testament and continuing to the present day, the attack upon man's sense of self and his love of God, has been a recurring theme of the enemy's attack on mankind.

Today, one area of man's vulnerability has metastasized into a world-wide epidemic of pornography. The power of this clever assault on mankind's relationship with God reaches even into many pulpits and ministries. The view in modern society is that pornography is a "normal and accepted" behavior that doesn't hurt anyone else. This is a clever lie that must be confronted and not tolerated. It is an orchestrated scheme of the enemy to subvert the design and purposes of God. It estranges the relationship one has with the Lord, thereby diminishing one's spiritual effectiveness.

"I will set nothing wicked before my eyes. I hate the work of those who fall away; It shall not cling to me." Psalms 101:3 (NKJV)

More subtle strongholds that can sabotage a person's relationship with God can be an obsession with making money, over-focusing on a talent, hobbies, sports activities, television, news media, other forms of entertainment or any one of the countless other distractions that supersede our relationship with God and the plan He has for our lives.

The battle against strongholds begins in the mind where the pre-eminence of Christ is declared and established. This is where the Word of God releases its power. When Jesus was tempted of the devil in the desert, He resisted and overcame the temptation using the Word of God. (Mt. 4: 4,7,10)

The journey from a self-centered and/or sin influenced life-style, to a God-influenced life is often difficult. Except for a few mentally-troubled souls, most people know right from wrong. They know it's wrong to hurt others or to steal from people. The fear of being caught or the consequences of wrong-doing usually keeps most people in check. An individual may be able to control blatantly acting out sinful thoughts and desires, but those sinful desires are there nevertheless, waiting for the chance to surface.

An analogy that demonstrates the multi-faceted nature of sin and the way to deal with it can be found in how we choose to deal with weeds in our lawn or garden. We can use a weed-trimmer to shorten the weeds to a visually appropriate level. This corresponds to the way we tend to deal with our self-centered sinful desires. We trim them back in order that we may be perceived as a socially-acceptable human being.

As in the case of using a weed-trimmer, the root is still there and just like the weed the sinful behavior will come back. Our sinful nature reasserts itself at the earliest opportunity.

We may be able to achieve some degree of success in controlling our sinful nature for a short period of time (weed-trimming). In so doing, we delay the corresponding consequences these behaviors eventually cause. The underlying problem continues to exist until the "root of the problem" or the sin, is addressed. In both the weed and the sin analogy, attacking the root of a spiritual stronghold yields the greatest success.

As Christian believers mature, they learn to **repent, renounce** and **disassociate** themselves from these distracting tactics and deceptive tools of the enemy, thereby **dislodging** their grip and influence. So how do we attack the root (the sin stronghold) in our lives?

The battle against the strongholds of the enemy is often difficult to overcome alone. It is more effectively accomplished with the involvement of **another mature believer**, i.e. Christian mentor, pastor, counselor, bible study leader, etc. who relies on and utilizes prayer **and the power of the Holy Spirit** to help break the stronghold's power.

Becoming accountable to a spiritual mentor is of great benefit in attaining and maintaining a consistent victorious spiritual walk. In much the same way that the power of an extortioner or blackmailer is broken when the shameful, illegal or inappropriate behavior of the victim is brought to the light, the power of the sins we have committed lose their hold over us when we face our sins and reveal our short comings to someone else.

"Confess your trespasses to one another, and pray for one another, that you may be healed. The effective, fervent prayer of a righteous man avails much." James 5:16 (NKJV)

Do not let **pride or fear** keep you from enlisting the help of a pastor or mature Christian who is expected to keep what you say in confidence and will believe with you to break the influence of the stronghold(s) in your life. This is where the power of **believer-agreement** and **deliverance** come into play. The involvement of the Holy Spirit is an absolute necessity in the effort to dislodge spiritual strongholds.

Jesus said, *"Yes, I am the vine; you are the branches. Those who remain in me, and I in them, will produce much fruit.* **For apart from me you can do nothing.***"* John 15:5 (NLT)

This battle tends not to be successful long-term if attempted in someone's own strength. The believer needs to submit to God's Holy Spirit as they engage in the stronghold battles of life.

"Therefore submit to God. Resist the devil and he will flee from you." James 4:7 (NKJV)

Very often at the beginning of the spiritual maturing process, a new believer will focus on the second part of this scripture and then wonder why the devil doesn't "flee" when they attempt to resist him. Once they begin to more fully discover the first part of that scripture, *"Therefore submit to God,"* and embrace them together, a whole new awareness and strategy on how to be successful in overcoming the devil results. Our success in resisting the devil is proportional to the degree to which we are submitted to God.

Questions:

1. On a scale from 0-10 (0 being least, 10 highest), how "submitted to God" are you?

2. What are the strongholds in your life and how do you plan to dislodge them?

Points to Consider:

Although there are many types of strongholds, there are three areas that maturing Christians must learn to deal with. They are tithing, un-forgiveness and pride. Learn to repent, renounce and disassociate from these distracting tactics and deceptive tools of the enemy, thereby dislodging their grip and influence.

CHAPTER TWENTY THREE
CHRISTIAN WEAPONS OF WAR

God is sovereign, all-powerful and fully capable of succeeding in every aspect of conflict with our adversary the devil. He doesn't necessarily need our help, but has made provision for mankind to "partner" with Him to set everything back in right order. Jesus made special weapons available to all who choose to believe in Him and engage in His mission, *". . . to destroy these works of the Devil."* 1 John 3:8 (NLT)

The greatest weapon we are to wield is **love.** It is His love that turns a sinner into a believer and a believer into one who sacrifices to spread the Good News of Jesus Christ. It is love that compels us to serve God and others.

Jesus said, *"'You must love the LORD your God with all your heart, all your soul, and all your mind.' This is the first and greatest commandment. A second is equally important: 'Love your neighbor as yourself.' The entire law and all the demands of the prophets are based on these two commandments."* Mt. 22:37-40 (NLT)

Consider Paul's writings describing the battle and nature of our adversary the devil and the necessity of being prepared and equipped with the full armor of God.

"Finally, my brethren, be strong in the Lord and in the power of His might. **Put on the whole armor of God**, *that you may be able to stand against the wiles of the devil.* **For we do not wrestle against flesh and blood, but against principalities, against powers, against the rulers of the darkness of this age, against spiritual hosts of wickedness in the heavenly places.** *Therefore take up the whole armor of God, that you may be able to withstand in the evil day, and* **having done all, to stand.** *Stand therefore, having* **girded your waist with truth**, *having* **put on the breastplate of righteousness,** *and having* **shod your feet with the preparation of the gospel of peace;** *above all,* **taking the shield of faith with which you will be able to quench all the fiery darts of the wicked one.** *And take the* **helmet of salvation, and the sword of the Spirit, which is the word of God; praying always with all prayer and supplication in the Spirit, being watchful** *to this end with all perseverance and supplication for all the saints-- and for me, that utterance may be given to me,* **that I may open my mouth boldly to make known the mystery of the gospel."** Eph. 6: 10-19 (NKJV)

Though I'd read it many times, I didn't really start to "get it" until the Lord gave me a slightly different vision of what He'd already covered in His Word. The visualization that opened my spiritual understanding occurred when

I perceived myself in a small boat in which I was making my way over "dangerous waters" of sin and evil.

In the bottom of the boat were leaks through which "sin" was slowly trying to seep in. On the one hand, they didn't seem like they were an imminent threat toward sinking the boat. It looked as though I could easily ignore them and still make my way merrily along.

Then my eyes were opened and I saw the absolute importance of **plugging all the holes** as quickly and as thoroughly as possible. Those seemingly minor leaks were a growing threat to me and my spiritual influence, **and they were actually hurting others.** It was clear that settling for less than totally sealing the boat was unacceptable.

Even though we may come to the point of understanding the importance of sealing the boat, this does not mean that the devil turns and runs. He still has a willing accomplice within us (our still active self-centered nature) and will try to keep some of the leaks flowing. He will use his weapons of lies and deceit to distract us from our mission to plug **all** the holes.

He'll even pat us on the back as we plug **almost all** of the holes. We look at how well we've done in some areas and put off plugging those last few holes. The "fiery darts" of the wicked one referenced in Scripture, and the "sin leaking into the boat" in my vision, are one and the same.

The way to deal with these subtle attacks of the enemy is in the Word of God. Consider this breakdown of the instructions for putting on the whole armor of God from Eph. 6: 10-19 (NKJV).

"Put on the whole armor of God,"
- Don't skimp, try to take a short cut or compromise.

"For we do not wrestle against flesh and blood, but against principalities, against powers, against the rulers of the darkness of this age, against spiritual hosts of wickedness in the heavenly places."
- Understand the spiritual realm of the battle and who you're fighting against.

"having done all, to stand."
- Get your spiritual armor in place and stand against **all** evil.

"gird your waist with truth."
- Guard your inner being with truth and nothing less. Settle in your mind that the Bible is the source of all truth.

"put on the breastplate of righteousness."
- Guard your heart and know it is God that you serve and represent.

> *"shod your feet with the preparation of the gospel of peace."*

- Study the Scriptures that they might do their good work within you and through you.

> *"taking the shield of faith with which you will be able to quench all the fiery darts of the wicked one."*

- Do not doubt or fear. Have faith in God and your faith in Him will overpower and quench the "fiery darts" (sin and temptation) of the wicked one.

> *"And take the helmet of salvation, and the sword of the Spirit, which is the word of God."*

- Your helmet of salvation represents your assurance of salvation. It is your defensive weapon guarding your mind, your hearing, your sight, etc. Your offensive weapon is the sword of the Spirit, the Word of God. Speak aloud what the Word of God says about your problems and challenges. Also, speak the Word of God and His promises into the lives of others as they face their challenges.

> *"praying always with all prayer and supplication in the Spirit."*

- Be in a prayerful state of mind with God always.

"being watchful."
- Be on guard for every clever trick of the enemy and also be open to the guiding unction of the Holy Spirit.

"that I may open my mouth boldly to make known the mystery of the gospel."
- Be ready to share the Gospel confidently as did Paul and the other Apostles.

And the Apostle Paul's
marching orders
to us all.
"But you be watchful in all things, endure afflictions, do the work of an evangelist, fulfill your ministry."
2 Timothy 4:5 (NKJV)

When Jesus described His purpose *"to destroy the works of the devil"* which is also our command, He did not intend for us to leave any of the leaks in our boat unplugged.

It's time to:
  declare war,
    put on the full armor of God,
      plug every hole, and
        quench every fiery dart of the enemy.

IT'S TIME TO
FULLY ENGAGE IN THE BATTLE!

Jesus confirmed another weapon to be used in spiritual warfare. It is the **power of believer-agreement** in prayer.

"Again I say to you that if two of you agree on earth concerning anything that they ask, it will be done for them by My Father in heaven. For where two or three are gathered together in My name, I am there in the midst of them." Mt. 18:19-20 (NKJV)

The **power of believer-agreement** is a powerful tool God has placed in the hands of believers, to partner with other believers and access the power of God. However, it does not give the power or authority to contradict the character or purposes of God or to violate the Word of God. It allows us to be intimately involved in God's dealings with man and also to influence the spiritual realm.

Prayer and believer-agreement are often used to impact the physical world in the area of healing. It also extends into the spiritual realm in the area of **blocking and binding** the activities of demonic forces and **loosing or releasing Godly influence** in the spiritual as well as in the earthly realms. Jesus' ministry on earth included the physical healing of the afflicted and their deliverance from demonic influences.

Fasting, the practice of drawing closer to God by the temporary limiting of physical stimulation and indulgence (food or any other craving of the body), is another weapon given to believers to draw closer to God. As disappointing as it may seem, fasting without prayer is not really fasting. It's called dieting!

The intent and purpose of the weapons that God has made available to us in this battle against spiritual darkness are first to assist *us* in our own personal battles. They are also made available to assist us as we engage in spiritual warfare on behalf of others. **God-given spiritual gifts** and weapons are very useful in helping to win the unsaved (the lost) into the "family of God."

As described in Matthew chapter twelve, Jesus was informed that His family had arrived and wanted to talk to him. Instead of jumping up to help bring His family members in, He took this time to instruct those present as well as all future generations, about what is necessary to be included in the eternal family of God.

Then one said to Him (Jesus), *"Look, Your mother and Your brothers are standing outside, seeking to speak with You."* But He answered and said to the one who told Him, *"Who is My mother and who are My brothers?"* And He stretched out His hand toward His disciples and said, *"Here are My mother and My brothers! For whoever does the will of My Father in heaven is My brother and sister and mother."* Mt. 12: 46-50 (NKJV)

Believers who do the will of God are **family** to Jesus. Jesus has done His part. He proved His love for man when He willingly sacrificed Himself for all mankind. The question for us becomes, *"What am I willing to do about it?"*

Many effective Christians learn to rely on and use a "prayer list." This begins by placing those people and issues of concern on a list for which they review and pray about daily. Some people and items on the list are there but for a season, while others are almost permanent entries on their list. These near-permanent entries often include spouses, children, parents, relatives, close friends, co-workers, pastors, community and national leaders, etc.

A prayer list is a great tool and reference with which to intercede on the behalf of others, in order that God might move in their life in a positive way.

In addition to seeing God answering these prayer list concerns, many people who remain faithful to this intercessory prayer practice often report God's hand of favor extending into their own life. It's as though God blesses those who pray faithfully for others, in addition to moving in a positive way in the lives of those being prayed for.

Again it is worth repeating, *"Our greatest weapon against the enemy is love."* God's greatest desire is first for us to love Him and then for us to love others and help bring them into His eternal family.

There is a saying that goes, *"Your life is God's gift to you. What you do with it, is your gift to God."* The world teaches us to render evil for evil and to seek revenge for evil committed against us. The Bible gives us a better way.

"Do not be overcome by evil, but overcome evil with good." Romans 12:21 (NKJV)

Questions:

1. What are the spiritual gifts and weapons identified in this chapter?

2. Which ones do you feel God has made available to you?

3. How are you using these God-given gifts and weapons to reach the lost and encourage other believers?

Point to consider:

Yes, it is written, *"Be diligent to present yourself approved to God, a worker who does not need to be ashamed, rightly dividing the word of truth."* 2 Timothy 2:15 (NKJV)

Do not forget love however, lest all your effort and learning becomes nothing more than a clanging cymbal.

CHAPTER TWENTY FOUR
ONCE SAVED, ALWAYS SAVED?

Although the subject was touched on previously, there is a doctrine and belief that is too important to not understand fully. Many individuals place their faith and hope in it and some scriptures seem to support it. For those who do not believe in it, there are other scriptures that seem to invalidate the **once-saved, always-saved** doctrine. They espouse the danger of entrusting one's eternal destiny to it.

A little deeper look into the Word of God helps bring clarity to this often divisive issue. Once carefully examined, these two seemingly diametrically opposed perspectives on "eternal security" are not as different as commonly believed.

"Once-saved, always saved" proponents are quick to reference Jesus' words:

"And I give them eternal life, and they shall never perish; neither shall anyone snatch them out of My hand. My Father, who has given them to Me, is greater than all; ***and no one is able to snatch them out of My Father's hand.'"*** John 10:28-29 (NKJV)

Indeed, there is eternal security for those who truly accept (**confess**) Jesus' death and resurrection, (**believe**) in His sacrifice and lordship and (**repent**) walk away from their sins. However, there are many other scriptures that indicate the dire fate of those **who do not really**

believe, do not really repent or who walk away from God after having experienced His goodness.

One problem with the "once-saved, always-saved" doctrine is that for some it is perceived in terms of **confessing only,** as the main and only necessary requirement to be granted access to eternal life in heaven. When someone back-slides or otherwise departs the faith, those believing in the once-saved doctrine are quick to say, *"They weren't really saved in the first place."* It is not our place to "judge" their salvation but we can discern much from their actual behavior subsequent to their profession of faith.

The more mature members of those denominations who teach the "once-saved, always-saved" doctrine understand the overall necessity of the key elements of **believing** and **repenting**.

The problem with promoting the "once-saved, always-saved" doctrine is the unintended fruit that it can produce. Some people who never fully engage have a, *"You mean all I have to do is say I accept Jesus and I get to go to heaven? - Sure, I'll do that"* mentality.

The Bible gives strong warnings for those who think that **repenting** is not necessary. Remember also, the demons believe but will not be re-admitted to heaven just for their believing.

Jesus said, ... *"No, **and I tell you again that unless you repent, you will perish, too.**"* Luke 13:2-5 (NLT)

*"For it is by **believing** in your heart that you are made right with God, and it is by **confessing** with your mouth that you are saved."* Romans 10:10 (NLT)

*"For the kind of sorrow God wants us to experience leads us away from sin and results in salvation. There's no regret for that kind of sorrow. **But worldly sorrow, which lacks repentance, results in spiritual death.**"* 2 Cor. 7:10 (NLT)

Acknowledging our **sin**, **believing** and accepting Jesus' sacrifice as payment for our sin and **repenting** (turning away from our sin), are the guideposts to real biblical salvation.

Imagine if only 5% of those who embrace this doctrine fall into the *"never really saved in the first place"* category. Very often these *"never really saved in the first place"* people (according to the once-saved proponents), appear abandoned by their denomination with little or no effort to win them back. Wouldn't Jesus want His true disciples (regardless of their current denomination) to reach out and expend considerable effort to bring those wandering souls into the *"really saved"* family of God?

Jesus said, "What do you think? If a man has a hundred sheep, and one of them goes astray, does he not leave the ninety-nine and go *to the mountains to seek the one that is straying? And if he should find it, assuredly, I say to you, he rejoices more over that sheep than over the ninety-nine that did not go astray."* Mt. 18:12-13 (NKJV)

God does not want anyone to suffer eternal destruction. He places the responsibility of reaching the unsaved on all true disciples of Christ. When we allow these *"never really saved in the first place"* (according to the once-saved doctrine) or those who have *"departed the faith"* (backslidden in non-once-saved denominations), to live their lives in danger of dying in their obvious unrepentant condition and never challenge their unacceptable worldly behavior or lifestyle, **their blood so to speak is on our hands.** Judging them instead of a sincere effort to love them and win them either back to or for the first time into the Kingdom of God, renders judgment unto ourselves.

"Brethren, if a man is overtaken in any trespass, you who are spiritual restore such a one in a spirit of gentleness, considering yourself lest you also be tempted. Bear one another's burdens, and so fulfill the law of Christ." Gal. 6:1-2 (NKJV)

The body of Christ would be better served if there was less time spent debating the "once saved, always saved" doctrine and more time actually going after (**restoring**) all those that are spiritually adrift.

A story once told by an old preacher helps illustrate the potential danger of the once-saved, always-saved doctrine. The story is about a wealthy man who lived in a very nice house located near the top of a mountain. One day the man's chauffer died and the wealthy man was forced to seek a replacement. On the day of the new chauffer interviews, many potential drivers waited outside. They were brought in one by one.

When the first candidate entered, the wealthy man inquired of the potential driver, *"Sir, you know the winding road that leads up to this house. I was wondering, how close to the outside edge of the road do you think you can drive and still be driving safely?"* The man thought for a minute and replied. *"Oh, I think I can get about a foot or so close to the edge and still be pretty safe."* The wealthy man thanked him and went on to the next potential driver. The afternoon progressed with one driver after another giving his answer to the wealthy man's question. Their answers varied from a few inches to as much as two feet.

Finally, one driver entered and was asked the same question. The driver looked a little disappointed as he began to sense he was not going to be selected, because of the answer he was about to give. Nevertheless, he gave his answer. *"Sir, I think you will probably need to keep looking for someone else, for you see, when I drive up that winding mountain road, I like to keep far away from the outside edge and as close to the mountain as possible."* Immediately the wealthy man stood up and said, *"You're hired!"*

It is a good story to consider when we try to imagine which kind of life and what kind of people Jesus is returning for. Is He coming for the person who is living on the edge and as close to the world as possible, while keeping God at arm's length away? Or is He coming for people who are striving to keep as close to Him as possible (the mountain) and far away from the world and all its temptations and dangers (the edge of the cliff)?

It is foolish to think you can live your life distant from God and as worldly as you want, **without repenting** and turning away from your sin, **and yet dance your way merrily into heaven** because of a quick prayer once said, but never actually lived out. After all, why would God welcome someone to be with Him for all eternity in heaven when that person chose not to serve Him or spend time with Him while they were here on earth?

Remember Jesus' words of warning to those who live their lives distant from God . . . . *"And then I will declare to them, **'I never knew you**; depart from Me, you who practice lawlessness!"* Mt. 7:21-23 (NKJV)

Another sobering scripture that should awaken our spiritual understanding concerning our spiritual walk and eternal destiny comes from the Apostle Paul.

*"But I discipline my body and bring it into subjection, lest, when I have preached to others, I myself should become **disqualified**."* 1 Cor. 9:27 (NLT)

When so great a teacher and disciple of Christ as was the Apostle Paul suggests that he needed to keep *his* spiritual house in order so as to avoid being **disqualified,** it might be wise for us to realize there looms great consequences for those who take lightly their **believing,** their **repenting** or if it occurs, their **backsliding** (departing the faith).

Our confession of faith is the first step to salvation of the soul. It is at this point that the soul of man begins to come into agreement with the Word of God. This journey can have many twists and turns, much like the winding road in the story.

During this life-long journey, many may take what appears to be the more worldly and exciting path (the edge of the cliff). True believers however, realize it's a lot safer and much wiser to choose the path and purposes of God and continually **stay close to the mountain.**

Questions:

1. On the winding road of life, what kind of spiritual driver have you been?

2. What are three basic guideposts of salvation?

3. Briefly share your view of the "once-saved, always-saved" doctrine.

Points to consider:

God does not want anyone to suffer eternal destruction. He places the responsibility of reaching the unsaved on all true Disciples of Christ.
"And you must show mercy to those whose faith is wavering. Rescue others by snatching them from the flames of judgment. Show mercy to still others, but do so with great caution, hating the sins that contaminate their lives." Jude 22-23 (NLT)

CHAPTER TWENTY FIVE
A TALE OF TWO NATIONS
(How did everything get so messed up?)

The Middle East and Israel are the major focal points on planet earth. Israel is surrounded and confronted by their age-old sworn enemy, the combined Islamic Arab nations. The desire and intention of extremist fundamental Islam is to destroy all Jews and to drive the nation of Israel into the sea. They want to claim Israel, the land that God promised and gave to His chosen people the Jews.

Some biblical scholars believe that the mark of the beast (666), referenced in the Bible in the book of Revelation is actually an associative acronym for radical Islam. Given the ongoing and deep-seeded jihad (holy war) that's in progress against Israel and the Jews, they may at least in part be right. This holy war extends to Christians, also considered by Muslims (Islam) as infidels, a term Muslims use for all non-Muslim/Islamic believers.

Radical Islam is exploding across the world. Christians and even moderate Muslims are being persecuted, kidnapped, beheaded and forced from their respective homelands by radical Islamists.

In order to better understand the times we are living in, it's important to understand a story that begins in the first book of the Bible, Genesis.

In this story, God begins to lay the foundation for the end-time conflict that we are beginning to see unfold in our current generation. This ancient conflict begins with the story of Abraham. It is of great significance and importance in understanding the chaos and turmoil we see today.

Abraham's wife Sarah despaired over having no children with Abraham. Failing to wait on God's plan and His promise to give them a child, they came up with their own plan. Sarah suggested that Abraham take her Egyptian handmaiden Hagar and conceive a child with her. Abraham did. As time passed, there was growing animosity between Sarah and Hagar and eventually Hagar found herself seeking refuge in the wilderness.

God heard the cry of Hagar, had compassion and sent a ministering angel to her in the desert. God made a promise to Hagar.

"I will give you more descendants than you can count." And the angel also said, *"You are now pregnant and will give birth to a son. You are to name him Ishmael (which means 'God hears'), for the LORD has heard your cry of distress."* Genesis 16: 10-11 (NLT)

Ishmael is sometimes referred to as the **child of the flesh,** meaning he was the result of man's (Abraham and Sarah) plan to be fruitful. For many centuries the descendants of Ishmael flourished and multiplied to become a mass of disorganized tribes and factions. These groups began to become more organized when Muhammad (April 26, 570–June 8, 632) founded Islam and introduced the teachings which would later become the holy book of Islam, the Quran (or sometimes written as Koran).

Following a bitter struggle with the pagan tribes of Arabia, Muhammad and his group of nearly 10,000 followers conquered Mecca and established Islam, which would become the dominant religion of the Arab, Persian (modern-day Iran) world. Muhammad died shortly after this conquest, yet his followers (descendants of Ishmael) populated the area and today comprise what is known as the Arab/Islamic nations. These Arab nations, marked by centuries of conflict between themselves as well as with outsiders, are the fulfillment of the Bible's description of Ishmael's descendants, *"He will raise his fist against everyone, and everyone will be against him. Yes, he will live in open hostility against all his relatives."* Gen 16:12 (NLT)

The teachings in the Quran are the inspiration behind the militant faction of Islam that we now see spreading across the globe. The ultimate goal of Islam is to conquer the world both spiritually and politically.

After Ishmael was born, God again spoke about His promise to Abraham and Sarah. God told Abraham that he and his wife Sarah would conceive a child, Isaac **the child of promise**. His descendants would become a great (Hebrew) nation.

>   When Abram was ninety-nine years old, the LORD appeared to him and said, "I am El-Shaddai—'God Almighty.' Serve me faithfully and live a blameless life. I will make a covenant with you, by which I will guarantee to give you countless descendants."
>   At this, Abram fell face down on the ground. Then God said to him, "This is my covenant with you: I will make you the father of a multitude of nations! What's more, I am changing your name. It will no longer be Abram. Instead, you will be called Abraham, for you will be the father of many nations.
>   I will make you extremely fruitful. Your descendants will become many nations, and kings will be among them! I will confirm my covenant with you and your descendants after you, from generation to generation.
>   This is the everlasting covenant: I will always be your God and the God of your descendants after you. **And I will give the entire land of Canaan, where you now live as a foreigner, to you and your descendants. It will be their possession forever, and I will be their God."** Gen. 17:1-8 (NLT)

>   Then God said to Abraham, "Regarding Sarai, your wife—her name will no longer be Sarai. From now on her name will be

Sarah. And I will bless her and give you a son from her! Yes, I will bless her richly, and she will become the mother of many nations. Kings of nations will be among her descendants."

Then Abraham bowed down to the ground, but he laughed to himself in disbelief. "How could I become a father at the age of 100?" he thought. "And how can Sarah have a baby when she is ninety years old?" So Abraham said to God, "May Ishmael live under your special blessing!" **But God replied, "No—Sarah, your wife will give birth to a son for you. You will name him Isaac, and I will confirm my covenant with him and his descendants as an everlasting covenant.**

As for Ishmael, I will bless him also, just as you have asked. I will make him extremely fruitful and multiply his descendants. He will become the father of twelve princes, and I will make him a great nation. **But my covenant will be confirmed with Isaac, who will be born to you and Sarah about this time next year."** *When God had finished speaking, he left Abraham.* Gen. 17:15-22 (NLT)

In the New Testament of the Bible, the Apostle Paul makes reference to Abraham's son Isaac and the covenant God made through Isaac and his descendants, the people to which the covenant extends. Paul said,

"Well then, has God failed to fulfill his promise to Israel? No, for not all who are born into the nation of Israel are truly members of God's people! Being descendants of Abraham doesn't make them truly Abraham's children. For the Scriptures say, "Isaac is the son through whom your descendants will be counted," though Abraham had other children, too. This means that Abraham's physical descendants are not necessarily children of God. Only the children of the promise (the descendants of Isaac) *are considered to be Abraham's children."* Romans 9:6-8 (NLT)

God made His covenant and intention known to Abraham in the first book of the Bible, Genesis. Around 2,000 years ago God reaffirmed His covenant through Abraham's descendant Isaac (the child of promise) in the writings of Paul the Apostle. Isaac's bloodline includes Jesus, and then further extends to Christians by adoption, due to the redemptive work of Jesus.
Islam did not even come into being until nearly 600 years after Paul's New Testament writings. Basic research on the Jewish claim to the land in Israel compared to the Islamic claim reveals the authenticity of the Jewish claim, and the illegitimacy of the Islamic claim.

As tension continues to escalate between "moderate conventional Islamist" and the "radical jihadist", the effort to successfully confront the error of Islam is complicated. The truth of the gospel of Jesus Christ when properly presented can accomplish what years of debate and conflict never could.

The problem, even for the peace loving Muslim, is that Jesus has been cleverly and falsely included in the Islamic teachings they have already been exposed to. In their teachings they have included Jesus as one of their great prophets. They go on to teach that Muhamad came after Jesus as the Last and Greatest Prophet, thereby denying Jesus' deity and supreme authority. Muslims are therefore much more resistant to consider the truth of Christianity and the error of Islam.

This does not mean that attempting to reach Muslims with the truth should be abandoned. However, the adversarial confrontation about the religion and god they have been exposed to will likely be ineffective. This can be a delicate endeavor and needs to be a prayerful, Holy Spirit lead undertaking.

Regardless of, or in addition to the many suspicious signs concerning Islam as an anti-God end-time entity, there is yet another great sign or event that will be a forerunner to the prophesied end-time conflict. It has to do with the "great falling away" from the true Gospel of Jesus Christ that must take place before the end comes. (II Thess. 2: 3)

It is anticipated that this "falling away" will come about in the form of a man-orchestrated global effort to unite the so-called "Christian church" under one banner. It will look appealing for a variety of reasons **but will not be a "Holy Spirit of God" led effort.** It will appeal to many in the worldwide body of believers because it will address the fundamental desire to belong. However, it will not be solidly built on the sacrificial gospel of Jesus Christ with a driving concern for the salvation of the lost.

In these last days this global apostate church will deceive many with its offer of inclusion and social acceptance, while the true church will be busy winning souls into His kingdom.

Questions:
1. According to the Bible explain who was the "child of flesh" and who was the "child of promise." Why are they referred in this way?
2. Who are the rightful heirs to the land of Israel? Why?

Point to consider:
Throughout history, true Disciples of Truth have been challenged to rise up and against every work of the enemy. Today, this includes radical Islam, perversion in the church, and the subtle societal pressure to accept ungodliness.

CHAPTER TWENTY SIX
GOD'S PEOPLE PERSECUTED

Through the centuries following Jesus' ministry on earth, Jews as well as Christians have been persecuted for their faith. In World War II millions of Jews were killed in an all-out effort to exterminate them as a race. Today in ever-increasing intensity Christians world-wide are being persecuted, tortured and killed for their belief in Jesus Christ to the point that Christians are now "the most persecuted religious group on earth." This attempted genocide of both Jews and Christians was fueled, and continues to be fueled, by Satan's hatred of God and His people.

Today, many Jews have a conflicted relationship with God. On the one hand, they know themselves to be God's chosen people through whom God revealed Himself in the Old Testament. On the other hand, they have trouble with God having allowed them to endure such severe persecution throughout history. It is somewhat ironic that mainstream Jewish and many current day Israelis do not consider Jesus as Messiah, when in reality the suffering and great persecution they have endured over the centuries is because of Him.

The descendants of Abraham from his two half-brother-sons, **Isaac the child of God's promise** (represented by the Jews and Christians by adoption) and **Ishmael the child of the flesh** (represented by Arabs and radical Islam), are locked in a seemingly unresolvable conflict. The Jews cannot give up land given to them by God without grave consequences. Irrespective of the current day counterfeit Palestinian claim to Jerusalem, the center and "capital" of the Jewish people is, and has been Jerusalem, for over three thousand years.

"So the LORD made a covenant with Abram that day and said, "I have given this land to your descendants, all the way from the border of Egypt to the great Euphrates River—" Gen. 18:15 (NLT)

The Arabs (consisting of Arab and Persian heritage) have made a similar claim to this same piece of land. God **did not promise the descendants of Ishmael the land** which He'd already given to the Jews. He did, however, fulfill His promise to make the descendants of Ishmael a great nation. (Gen.17: 20)

It is fairly easy to see the difference in the historical belief of the Bible and Jewish tradition, as compared to the Islamic belief and tradition. The Bible teaches that Isaac was the offered sacrifice before God by Abraham, while Islam teaches that Ishmael was offered as a sacrifice before God by Abraham. Both groups feel their claim to Abraham's legacy is authentic. Some within Islam even teach that Jesus was a Muslim, even though Islam did not even exist until nearly 600 years after Jesus' time on earth.

According to the Bible, Christians are challenged to reach the entire world peacefully and with love and to bring the lost to a saving and intimate relationship with God, through belief in Jesus Christ. According to the Quran, Muslims are instructed to conquer the world and cause all people to submit to Islam, if need be forcibly and with violence. **These two religions and belief systems are on a collision course.**

In the bible book of Revelation God describes the defeat of Satan and his followers. Jesus and His followers (Christians) will emerge victorious at the culmination of the end-time events.

The essence of this conflict can be simplified down to its core elements. **It is the doctrine of love vs. the doctrine of hate.** On the one hand, we see Jews and Christians who want to live in peace. We also see Christians reaching out to the world with God's love. Just prior to His death, Jesus instructed his followers,

"So now I am giving you a new commandment: Love each other. Just as I have loved you, you should love each other. Your love for one another will prove to the world that you are my disciples." John 13:34-35 (NLT)

On the other hand, we see a growing Arab/Islamic holy war that is committed to exterminate all Jews and kill all who refuse to submit to Islam. There has been and continues to be, violent competition and bloodshed between Islamic factions. They are however, united in their end-time persecution of Jews and Christians. In this regard, they will surely cooperate with one another as they spread their hatred world-wide from Israel to the rest of the western civilized world.

Jews and Christians are not opposed to living and co-existing with other nations, peoples or countries. The extremist Islamic factions, driven by spiritually demonic forces, are unwilling and incapable of doing likewise. They are a major factor in the end-time persecution of God's people.

The authenticity of the gods of these two diametrically opposed religions is evident. Allah, the god of the Islamic faith promises fleshly and lustful rewards to followers. They are trained to use forced submission on infidels (all non-Muslim followers) utilizing terrorist activities including beheadings, bombings, kidnappings, and torture.

Remember Jesus' warning, *". . . yes, the time is coming that whoever kills you will think that he offers God service. And these things they will do to you because they have not known the Father nor me. But these things I have told you, that when the time comes, you may remember that I told you of them."* John 16:2-3 (NKJV)

When Islamic terrorists do these prophesied things, the inherent weakness and falseness of the Islamic god is obvious. Hate is the motivation of Islam.

God Almighty, Creator of the universe, the God of Abraham, Isaac and Jacob of the Bible to whom Jews and Christians ascribe, does not nor does He need to, force anyone to accept Him. He loves all mankind and is the ultimate authority concerning all things. Love is the motivation of true Christianity.

"No eye has seen, no ear has heard, and no mind has imagined what God has prepared for those who love him." 1 Corinthians 2:9 (NLT)

Questions:
1. What is the difference between the God of the Bible and Allah, the god of Islam?

2. Why are Jews and by adoption Christians, being persecuted today?

Point to consider:
The essence of the conflict between Christianity and Islam can be simplified down to its core elements. It is the doctrine of love vs. the doctrine of hate. **What if the followers of Jesus were as committed to spreading the truth of the gospel of Jesus Christ as are the Islamic terrorists who lay down their lives for their false god?**

CHAPTER TWENTY SEVEN
THE COUNTERFEIT GOD

According to the Bible, when the Israeli/Islamic conflict escalates there will emerge a false prophet and a charismatic leader, **the anti-Christ**. This leader will appear to miraculously bring peace to the Middle East. He will convince Israel to make peace with the surrounding Islamic groups. It is speculated that this peace will include an agreement that involves Israel giving up the land that was promised and given to them by God. This will be a strong sign that the end-time **Great Tribulation** (seven-year period of global turmoil) is imminent.

"For then there will be great tribulation, such as has not been since the beginning of the world until this time, no, nor ever shall be." Mt. 24:21 (NKJV)

"But concerning the times and the seasons, brethren, you have no need that I should write to you. For you yourselves know perfectly that the day of the Lord so comes as a thief in the night. For when they say, "Peace and safety!" then sudden destruction comes upon them, as labor pains upon a pregnant woman. And they shall not escape. But you, brethren, are not in darkness, so that this Day should overtake you as a thief. 1 Thessalonians 5:1-4 (NKJV)

Ultimately, the anti-Christ will declare himself to be God and demand that mankind submit and worship him. Those who submit to him will receive the **mark of the beast,** possibly some mark or computer chip inserted in their right hand or in their forehead. This will be a sign of their submission. They will be allowed to live. Those who refuse to accept the mark and **do not deny their belief in Jesus Christ** will be put to death, resulting in their entry into heaven and into God's presence for all eternity.

"He was granted power to give breath to the image of the beast, that the image of the beast should both speak and cause as many as would not worship the image of the beast to be killed. He causes all, both small and great, rich and poor, free and slave, to receive a mark on their right hand or on their foreheads, and that no one may buy or sell except one who has the mark or the name of the beast, or the number of his name. Here is wisdom. Let him who has understanding calculate the number of the beast, for it is the number of a man: His number is 666." Rev. 13:15-18 (NKJV)

The rise of the false prophet and the anti-Christ is a cleverly-crafted counterfeit of God's plan. Using supernatural powers, Satan's servants will perform seemingly miraculous signs and wonders that will deceive many.

One example of a present-day clever plot by Satan to deceive man is the recent false doctrine and teaching of **Chrislam**. This so-called combination of Christianity and Islam is an abomination that will deceive some who are not well-grounded in their faith. God will not share His glory with Allah or any other supposed deity. In the Bible God makes this very clear.

*"He showed you these things so you would know that the L*ORD* is God **and there is no other**."* Deut. 4:35 (NLT)

". . for you shall worship no other god, for the Lord, whose name is Jealous, is a jealous God." Ex. 34:14 (NKJV)

Jesus said, *"Then if anyone tells you, 'Look, here is the Messiah,' or 'There he is,' don't believe it. For false messiahs and false prophets will rise up and perform signs and wonders so as to deceive, if possible, even God's chosen ones. Watch out! I have warned you about this ahead of time!"* Mark 13:21-23 (NLT)

Politically, the exact positioning of the main end-time players is a mystery. The question often asked is, "Where is the United States in all of these end-time prophecies?" Why isn't the world's most powerful nation mentioned in this prophesied end-time conflict? Most Bible theologians agree that according to the Bible the involvement of the United States in the end-time conflict is curiously absent. Some theologians believe and teach that the United States is actually the mystery Babylon mentioned in the Bible and will be effectively destroyed and unable to play a role in the end-time conflict.

The list of possible reasons for the United States' non-involvement is left to speculation since the Bible does not give us a clear explanation. Whether it will be a natural disaster, civil war, plague, political take-over or just a reluctance to be involved, the United States does not appear to be a part of the approaching Middle East end-time conflict in any definitive way.

The emerging, major end-time players appear to be part of two major groups. On the one side you have the Jews (Israel) and Christians. On the other side you have Islam and possibly to a certain extent, Communism. Islam is driven by its desire to exterminate the Jews and destroy the United States. They want to eventually conquer the entire world in the name of Allah (Islam).

Major Islamic terrorist groups include Hamas, the Muslim Brotherhood, al-Qaeda, ISIS or ISIL, DAASH, Hezbollah, Boko Haram. A partial list of a few of the lesser known regional Islamic extremist groups operating worldwide include: Abu Sayyaf (Philippines), Aden-Abyan Islamic Army (Canada, UK), al-Gama'a al-Islamiyya (Russia, UK), al-Gama'a al-Islamiyya (Libya), East Turkestan Islamic Movement, Army of Islam (Gaza, Israel), Students Islamic Movement of India (India), Jamiat-e Islami (Russia), Al-Shabaab (Somalia). Within the Islamic nations surrounding Israel, two competing groups vie for the position of being the dominant Islamic influence; the Shia and Sunni factions.

Early in the development of Islam, a division arose because of the assassination of Husayn ibn Ali, Muhammed's grandson in the seventh century. This estranged the relationship of the Shia sect currently comprised of roughly 15% of the world's 1.6 billion Muslims. This group believes that the legitimate leadership of Islam must be through Muhammed's blood line. Iran and those nations approximate to and influenced by Iran, ascribe to the Shia teachings.

Sunni, currently comprising approximately 85% of the world's 1.6 billion Muslims, do not look at the Shia leaders as the legitimate spiritual and political leaders of Islam. Though there have been several centuries of relative peace between these two sects, there has been recent growing distrust and animosity between them. Their conflict destabilizes the Middle East and through increasingly militant Islam, the entire world.

Iran's quest to obtain nuclear bomb-making capability has been of great concern considering Iran is the main supporter of terrorism world-wide. The recent capability of North Korea to make and then deliver a nuclear bomb, and it's collusion with Iran in this area, is also of grave concern. Iran and North Korea have not lived up to the intended spirit of the major agreements they have made with the western world in recent times. Neither can be trusted.

If the civilized world is unsuccessful in keeping nuclear weapons away from Iran, and in preventing North Korea from perfecting their delivery capability of their existing and proven nuclear arsenal, a world held hostage by the threat of horrific consequences can be expected.

There are slight differences in the ideologies of the different Islamic extremists groups. They are untied however, in their desire to obliterate all other religions and establish Islam as the dominant religion of the world.

The anti-Israel, anti-Christian mindset inherent in Islamic extremism is a global fundamental ideology, regardless of which new Islamic terrorist-named group emerges as the leader of the effort at any particular moment. Assaults by militant Islam on all facets of the civilized and western world in the form of "lone-wolf" or sometimes called "home-grown" terrorist attacks, seemingly random killing sprees, attacks on public events, the police and military personnel, bombings etc., can be expected to escalate world-wide. These terrorist activities should be anticipated by the civilized world and appropriate countermeasures implemented.

Communism though largely an atheistic political entity, wants to destroy the United States who is viewed as their only remaining obstacle to world domination. It is also very possible that Russia may, in an attempt to appeal to the moralistic and nationalistic element of their own people, begin to promote a pro-Christian, anti-gay, anti-liberal sounding agenda while continuing their anti-capitalism rhetoric. This will not be a sincere effort to promote Christianity, but rather an attempt to gain the support of the more moral and conservative elements of their people and to disguise their real agenda; to promote Russian/communist expansion.

They may also, in an attempt to garner public support, institute an anti-radical Islamic position to distance themselves from radical Islam and to justify their intrusion into the Middle East in order to help bring stability to the region.

Militant Islam and the communists both want to control the world; Islam for spiritual and political reasons and Russia for military control and political supremacy. They are united in their desire to destroy the Judeo-Christian United States of America.

As the end-time Middle-East conflict approaches, Islam and Communism (both Russia and China) can be expected to tolerate each other, working together for the goal of world domination. The level of cooperation and involvement between these anti-true-God super-powers during the time of Israel's seeming last days is unknown.

What is known from the Bible, is that before all is lost, Jesus will return and intervene on behalf of Israel and Christians, His people. After the Great Tribulation, He will usher in the 1,000 year "millennial reign of Christ."

Though well-intentioned politicians and world leaders operate from a perspective that man can of his own ability bring about "peace on earth," this will not happen. This does not mean that believers and followers of Christ should abandon all hope or concern for the future. It just means that the preservation of our Judeo-Christian moral and spiritual beliefs is to be defended and that evil must be called out for what it is. Radical Islam and all other entities that threaten the Jewish/Christian alliance must be recognized and resisted, until Jesus returns and sets things in right order.

Today, extreme Islamic jihadists are attempting to re-establish a caliphate, an Islamic government ruled by the caliph who claims to be a legitimate successor to Muhammad and the leader of the Muslim nations.

Political leaders and nations that claim they will stamp out and destroy radical Islam are sadly mistaken. Islam is not a country that can be conquered. It is an ideology that is firmly rooted in its intent to destroy Israel and eventually all non-Muslim countries on earth. They will only be "defeated" when Jesus returns. Jesus, not any country or group of countries, defeats them and the demonic forces driving them.

Islam is one of the most successful fabrications Satan has ever devised. To date, it has been successful in deceiving over one billion people on the planet. It cleverly includes Jesus as one of the "great prophets", and then undermines His divinity by going on to reference Muhammad as "the last and greatest prophet." Even if every Islamic jihadist were to suddenly die, radical Islam would re-emerge in a few short years as new readers of the Quran would read its "conquer the world" commands and again wage war, terrorizing the civilized world. Though there are many so-called "good" Muslims, there is unfortunately the call to the "jihad" of radical Islam in the teachings of the Quran.

The non-Muslim world should resist every advance of Islamic intrusion into their countries. To allow the unchecked flow of Islamic influence into any country only provides an access point through which radical Islamic terrorists can infiltrate a community, a state or a nation.

This expansion is part of Islam's plan to take over a country and establish Sharia law (the legal moral code of Islam). This plan is well underway in European countries and other nations where the immigration of Muslims has not been appropriately vetted or gone unchecked altogether.

In many areas where highly Muslim infiltrated communities have been allowed to flourish, Sharia law has replaced the prior ruling law and order mechanism. In many of these communities the former government's police officers have designated these newly formed Sharia law areas as "no go" zones.

Unless a country or nation takes steps to curtail this unchecked infiltration of Muslim influence, the social structure of their communities will be in danger of falling under Sharia law. Failure to implement anti-Islamic intrusion steps will also increase their country's exposure to the significant damage that could be inflicted by the Islamic terrorists they have unknowingly allowed into their country.

An appropriate course of action to help stem the destabilizing effect of Islamic intrusion into a country is to pass laws making Sharia law in any form, illegal. Denying the entry of **radical Islamists** into a country is also an integral component of the larger strategy of preserving the government, social structure and moral fabric of every non-Muslim country.

Question:

1. Since Islam, Communism and Christianity all want to "win the world", who will succeed?

Point to consider: A true and willing disciple of Christ realizes that in this day and age, *"The night is far spent, the day is at hand. Therefore let us cast off the works of darkness, and let us put on the armor of light."* Rom. 13:12 (NKJV)

CHAPTER TWENTY EIGHT
THE RAPTURE & THE SECOND COMING

"Immediately after the tribulation of those days the sun will be darkened, and the moon will not give its light; the stars will fall from heaven, and the powers of the heavens will be shaken."
Matthew 24:29 (NKJV)

The seven-year Great Tribulation will cover the entire earth and is the time when the anti-Christ comes into power.

An event called the "rapture" of the church is another mysterious end-time event that many, but not all Biblical scholars teach. Rapture comes from the Greek word *"harpazo"* meaning to snatch or take away. Believers are brought to heaven by Jesus.

"For the Lord Himself will descend from heaven with a shout, with the voice of an archangel, and with the trumpet of God. And the dead in Christ will rise first. Then we who are alive and remain shall be caught up together with them in the clouds to meet the Lord in the air. And thus we shall always be with the Lord. Therefore comfort one another with these words.
I Thessalonians 4:16-18 (NKJV)

Some Bible scholars teach a **pre-tribulation rapture** which suggests that believers in Christ will be removed from the earth

before the tribulation and joined with Him, thereby allowing them to avoid the pain and suffering of the seven-year Great Tribulation period.

Others teach a **mid-tribulation rapture** which suggests believers will be raptured (caught up to be with the Lord) **half-way through** the seven-year period (at the 3½ year point).

Some others believe in a **post-tribulation rapture** which suggests that believers **must endure all seven** of the Great Tribulation years, and then be caught up to be with the Lord Jesus Christ.

Still others do not believe in the "rapture" concept in terms of either a pre, mid or post-tribulation event. They believe that somehow the "saved" will be joined with the Lord Jesus at the end of the age in some other inexplicable way.

Whether there will be a pre, mid, or post-tribulation rapture is not of paramount importance. What is of vital importance is to be **saved from the penalty of sin and living in a personal relationship with God** through belief in His Son the Lord Jesus Christ when He does return.

It is likewise of absolute importance **prior to Jesus' return,** to be in a saved relationship with God before a person dies due to any expected or unexpected cause.

The "second coming of Christ" and the "rapture" are two events that are often misunderstood and therefore taught incorrectly. These events as understood by many, are perceived as one and the same event. They are not.

According to rapture proponents, the rapture happens before the "second coming of Christ" and involves Jesus removing from the earth those believers who have chosen to accept and serve Him. The rapture event regardless of whether pre, mid, or post will need to be accomplished by, or at the culmination of the Great Tribulation. It involves the saved followers of Jesus meeting up with the Lord Jesus **in the air.**

The second coming of Christ is an event in which Jesus **physically returns to earth** to bring judgment. He will then establish the 1,000 year "millennial reign of Christ."

*"Then the Lord will go forth And fight against those nations, As He fights in the day of battle. And in that day His feet will stand on the Mount of Olives, Which faces Jerusalem on the east. And the Mount of Olives shall be split in two, From east to west . . . "*Zech.14: 3-4 (NKJV)

When Jesus does return to earth, He will defend Israel against the anti-Christ and his army that will be surrounding Israel. Satan will be defeated and thrown into the bottomless pit and eventually (1,000 years later) into the **lake of**

fire, which is prepared for him and his fallen angels.

"The devil, who deceived them, was cast into the lake of fire and brimstone where the beast and the false prophet are. And they will be tormented day and night forever and ever." Rev. 20:10 (NKJV)

There is another verse in the book of Revelation of particular note concerning the fate of Satan before he is finally cast into the eternal lake of fire.

*". . . and he cast him into the bottomless pit, and shut him up, and set a seal on him, so that he should deceive the nations no more till the thousand years were finished. But after these things **he must be released for a little while**."* Revelation 20:3 NKJV

Some believers early in their Christian walk have wondered, *"Why would God, after Satan's 1,000 years of time in the bottomless pit, allow him to be let out of his confinement?"*

Many theologians believe that this temporary release of Satan is designed for the people born during the 1,000 year millennial reign of Christ to somehow experience their time of temptation and testing by Satan. Having been born during the millennial reign of Christ, they will not have had to experience the temptation of disobedience that Satan tempted mankind with before Jesus' return. After his brief release, Satan will be cast **permanently** into the lake of fire with no chance of escape.

Question:

1. What is the difference between the "Rapture" and the "Second Coming of Christ?"

2. What does *the Bible say* a person must do to gain eternal life?

Points to consider:

Whether there will be a pre, mid, or post-tribulation rapture is not of paramount importance. What is of vital importance is to be saved from the penalty of sin and living in a personal relationship with God through belief in His Son the Lord Jesus Christ, when He does return.

It is likewise of absolute importance prior to Jesus' return, to be in a saved relationship with God before a person dies due to any expected or unexpected cause.

CHAPTER TWENTY NINE
THE GREAT WHITE HARVEST

Throughout history, God has forewarned His people of significant events about to take place. The great flood of Noah's time, the destruction of Sodom and Gomorrah and the first coming of Jesus the Messiah are three well-known examples.

In the Old Testament as well as in the New Testament God has given considerable warnings, descriptions and prophecies concerning Jesus' second coming. Terms like "the end of the age," "the end of the world," "the great tribulation" or "Armageddon" are often used today in reference to these end-time events.

Jesus spoke of the end-time age so that the people living during that age and serving God would not be caught unaware.

Jesus replied, *"Don't let anyone mislead you, for many will come in my name claiming, 'I am the Messiah.' They will deceive many. And you will hear of wars and threats of wars, but don't panic. Yes, these things must take place, but the end won't follow immediately. Nation will go to war against nation, and kingdom against kingdom. There will be earthquakes in many parts of the world, as well as famines. But this is only the first of the birth pains, with more to come."* Mark 13:5-8 (NLT)

Much of the world does not believe in Jesus' second coming nor do they really believe in His first coming. Many groups today discount and disbelieve that the holocaust of World War II actually happened. Amongst some factions of the world there are already groups that do not believe that the World Trade Center was attacked by terrorists on 9/11, believing that the 9/11 attack was actually an American governmental plot to demonize Islam and give justification to attack Muslim countries.

The devil's manipulation and negative influence has distorted the public's perception of reality and history. The devil has been actively undermining every facet of biblical Christianity for thousands of years.

Despite what world opinion, scientists, or any other learned source might teach, the Word of God (the Bible) well-describes man's rebellion, arrogance, pride and Jesus' return for those that accept Him as Lord. It also states that God will bring judgment upon all who do not believe in Jesus' death and resurrection which results in loving and serving Him.

"But God shows his anger from heaven against all sinful, wicked people who suppress the truth by their wickedness. They know the truth about God because he has made it obvious to them. For ever since the world was created, people have seen the earth and sky. Through everything God made, they can clearly see his invisible qualities—his eternal power and divine nature. So they have no excuse for not. Yes,

they knew God, but they wouldn't worship him as God or even give him thanks. And they began to think up foolish ideas of what God was like. As a result, their minds became dark and confused. **Claiming to be wise, they instead became utter fools.***"* Romans 1:18-23 (NLT)

One late-night moment as I reflected on all the injustice and evil in the world that man inflicts on his fellow man, I asked the question, *"Lord, what do You see in us* (mankind)?" Out of the stillness of night I heard Him answer, *"I see my Son."* It became clear that the mission of every believer, every disciple of truth, is to help as many people as possible *"see Jesus"* and to make Him the Lord of their life. It is also clear that time to make a difference is growing short.

Jesus described the season of the approaching end-time events. One need not look further than today's headlines to know that we are surely in the season of His return. With time growing short, every effort must be made to reach those who have not come to a saving and intimate relationship with God through Jesus Christ.

The Bible tells us in Romans 12 verse 3 that God has given everyone "a measure of faith." Initial faith is not something man needs to create or make up on his own. If this measure of faith is used as God intends, it will lead people to Him and then on to even greater faith.

"But without faith it is impossible to please Him, for he who comes to God must believe that

He is, and that He is a rewarder of those who diligently seek Him." Heb. 11:6 (NKJV)

The diligent pursuit and seeking of God is an obvious characteristic in the life of a true believer. Someone who professes or claims to be a Christian, but is not diligently pursuing God, may not have had a true conversion experience. These undercover or *never say anything about their faith* church attendees, may be more in doubt about God's actual existence than in faith that He actually does exist.

All through the centuries even back to the time of Jesus' first disciples, the question of when the biblically prophesied end-time events would occur has intrigued mankind. One does not need to be a seasoned bible scholar to sense the escalating global chaos that is currently permeating the entire planet.

Along with the approaching Great Tribulation comes "a season of harvest" (soul winning), the likes of which the world has never seen. This is not the time to be distracted with the cares and concerns of this present physical world which is soon to pass away. These are the days that many of the saints of olden times would have wanted to see. They would have given much to participate in the great end-time harvest season and to see Jesus return to earth to set things in right order.

The fields that are "white for harvest" (John 4:35) references the "unsaved" of the world. Yet how many inside the church are deceived or are not spiritually where they need to be? For those who sense God's calling in this season of salvation, the message is clear. The precious time left must not be wasted. Both the unsaved outside the church, as well as the "lukewarm" or uncommitted inside the church walls, need to be pursued for the cause of Christ. To do less cannot be justified by any Disciple of Truth.

"For God is not unjust. He will not forget how hard you have worked for him and how you have shown your love to him by caring for other believers, as you still do." Hebrews 6: 10 (NLT)

Question:

1. How will God bring judgment upon all who do not believe in Jesus Christ, do not honor His sacrifice and who have not chosen to love and serve Him?

2. What is one obvious characteristic in the life of a true believer?

Point to consider:

The future holds either "regret" for not having done all that you could for Christ or "rejoicing" with those you help make heaven their eternal home.

CHAPTER THIRTY
THE LIST

In the early morning twilight moments not so long ago, I found myself reflecting on the people in my life that I admire in a spiritual sense. I started listing their names and you may consider doing the same.

These people who comprised "my list" were first faithful in their obedience and love for Christ. Next, they were the humble, steady followers of Jesus; some called to do their good and helpful deeds behind the scenes or hidden in the shadows. Then, when noticed for their efforts they are quick to re-direct thanks given to them to God, to whom belongs all the praise, all the glory and all the honor for every good deed they had done.

The final criteria of my "spiritual heroes" list was them actively doing something to help win others into the kingdom of God, whether putting forth physical effort and time in prayer and/or being a "witness", or financially supporting those in the front lines doing the work of winning the lost.

As I went over my contact list there were many I included. I have already begun telling those on my list of my appreciation for their willingness to incur all the resistance that always comes against those who love God and are submitted to His purpose. As opportunities arise, I let those on my list know they are on my list of people that I look up to. It's emotionally moving to see the impact it has on these often unsung heroes, who in many cases have gone virtually unnoticed. It is a blessing and encouragement for them and in those moments, has also been a bit overwhelming for me.

After making several entries, God enlightened me on what I was actually doing. On a small scale, I was replicating what He is doing with all mankind. He has a list called the Lamb's Book of Life. It contains the names of those who are faithful in their obedience and love for Jesus Christ His Son.

Whether it's God's list or my list, each list includes those who "prefer others" over their own self-interest and worldly attention. Likewise their concern and burden for the lost and the expansion of God's kingdom, has resulted in a concerted effort to reach the unsaved, whether in action, financial support and/or intercessory prayer.

If you start a list of the spiritual heroes in your life and plan to let them know how they have been a positive influence in your spiritual walk, prepare for some emotional moments! The appreciation you share with them might be a few of the rare and infrequent acknowledgments they will receive for their efforts on this side of eternity.

If you embark on compiling your list, eventually you will suddenly find yourself wondering, *"Am I on anyone else's spiritual* heroes list? *Have I been conducting myself in such a manner that my love and appreciation of Christ is evident? Have I been haughty or acting spiritually aloof? Have I been the humble servant of Christ that He desires me to be? Have I really been concerned about winning the lost to Christ and actually doing something about it?"*

"Lord, help me to become and to be who you desire me to be, in order that I might help others become who You desire them to be."

Let this simple prayer be the prayer that guides your every step.

I hope you start your own "spiritual heroes" list, then let those individuals know of the impact they've made in your life and the appreciation you have for them.

Finally, it is my earnest hope that life finds you on the spiritual "heroes list" of many.

Spiritual challenge:

Prayerfully consider your list of "spiritual heroes." Begin sharing your appreciation with those on your list today. Make a point to be an encourager of all Disciples of Truth.

CHAPTER THIRTY ONE
THE VALLEY OF DECISION

*"Multitudes, multitudes in the valley of decision!
For the day of the Lord is near
in the valley of decision."*
Joel 3:14 (NKJV)

I heard this story or analogy years ago and used to call it "The Phone Call" story. A grey-headed preacher first told this and it's always stuck with me. It has been used on many occasions and is worth telling again.

This preacher was attempting to challenge a small group of young teens to step up and get the "Jesus issue" established in their lives. He told each to think about where they currently were in their life and then to imagine two very different paths from that point going forward.

In the first imagined path, he described them continuing in a lifestyle of pleasure seeking and self-centered pursuits. He suggested a variety of life style patterns that would fit the bill, ie. drinking, drugs, obsessing with pornography, over-focusing on sports, becoming controlled by being famous or financially successful with little thought to God's kingdom and His call to sacrifice. He listed many things that could become the life-controlling main focus in someone's life, displacing the pursuit of God's plan for their life.

Next, he asked them to imagine another version of themselves. The version where they decided to make the pursuit of God and His plan for their life the path they would follow, forsaking all the worldly distractions of life. I recall him using identical twins, who each made their own life choice after contemplating these two different imagined scenarios. Then he made it more personal as he explained that, of course, this actually applied to everyone hearing the story.

The old preacher continued, *"Now, somewhere in the future, maybe in 10 years, maybe next week, maybe next year there's going to be a phone call, or it could be a knock at the door. It really doesn't matter how the news comes, but it will be something like this, 'There's been a serious accident and your (husband, sister, mother, brother, son, daughter etc.,) is at the hospital – You better get here as quick as you can."*

"Now you (in both these imagined versions of you) hang up the phone and quickly grab a few things as you rush out the door. You both drive a little faster than you probably should toward the hospital as your minds race. The ominous words press down on you 'You better get here as fast as you can'. It doesn't sound good and you feel that the urgency of the call suggests you better get there quick before the loved one you care about passes on. You feel the tears trying to well up in

your eyes in both these two different versions of you racing toward the hospital."

The one version of you has been living a life apart from serving God. Your precious time has been spent on your work, pleasures, habits, hobbies, etc.

The two different versions of you reach the hospital and push your way through the emergency room doors. Both versions of you have been crying out to God, yet there is something very different about your pleas to heaven. The (not serving God you) is fearful, half crying in your plea, expressing regret for having been so distant and resistant to God. Your hope and expectation that God will hear your plea is almost non-existent. You feel regret for not having chosen to honor and live for Jesus as you should. You fear and expect the worst.

The other version of you, the one who has been trying to know and serve God as best you could enters the hospital, but something very different is taking place. Your heart is racing because someone you care about has been in a serious accident. But right there, even in the emotion of the moment, there is an air of expectancy within you. You have hope, and a knowing that the God you've grown to love and serve is with you, and hears your prayer. You are not a sobbing wreck in the midst of deep regret. You are not alone, because the Spirit of the living God is in you. You know He will see you through *this trying situation. You know that He, because of your prayers and faithfulness, will "hear" your petition. Just how He ultimately deals with the traumatic situation you're facing is His business. But you know that you will ultimately be okay with how it all turns out.*

Back to the phone call or knock at the door. Like it or not, believe it or not, it's coming. The decision we all have to make is, which version of ourselves and which path, are we going to take. Today you get to decide who you will be on that future day. Are you going to be the one weeping in regret, or the one boldly bursting through the doors of the hospital room, expecting the God you serve to show Himself strong? It's your choice."

For your own peace of mind, and in order that you become the spiritual warrior that the people you care about need you to be on that day, it is my hope and prayer that you choose wisely.

"Multitudes, multitudes in the valley of decision!
For the day of the Lord is near
in the valley of decision."
Joel 3:14 (NKJV)

CHAPTER THIRTY TWO
THE LAST CHAPTER

Jesus came and told his disciples, "I have been given all authority in heaven and on earth. Therefore, go and make disciples of all the nations, baptizing them in the name of the Father and the Son and the Holy Spirit. Teach these new disciples to obey all the Commands I have given you. And be sure of this: I am with you always, even to the end of the age."
Mt. 28:18-20 (NLT)

Jesus said to the people who believed in him, "You are truly my disciples if you remain faithful to my teachings. ***And you will know the truth, and the truth will set you free."***
John 8:31-32 (NLT)

Hopefully this book has informed you and encouraged you toward an intimate relationship with God through Jesus Christ. This is what God desires for your life. This plan is for you, and affects all the other people in your life within your sphere of influence. Your sphere of influence is comprised of all the people in and connected to your life.

What exactly is our influence? It's made up of what we say, what we do, what others see us condone or refuse to condone. It's what we do with our money or how we spend our time.

Actually, our influence is a multi-faceted and often overlooked and sadly underappreciated commodity.

Our influence is the vehicle and means by which we partner with God to achieve His plan for our life, and also the lives of those around us.

You might be a fairly mature believer already but not as fully committed to the Lord's plan for your life as you could and should be. You might be relatively new to Christianity, find yourself reading this book and are almost convinced that you should **accept** Jesus as Lord and Savior, **repent** or turn away from your sins and fully **commit** to God's plan and purpose for your life.

Take a moment to visualize where you are in your spiritual walk. Imagine the future plan and destiny that God has for you as a doorway or gateway. Aside from the obstacles, distractions and hindrances that our adversary and his demonic followers present, there is one other hindrance or entity that is the major obstacle standing in the way of your breakthrough with God.

The entity that stands at the gateway of our spiritual breakthrough is none other than our own self-centered nature. It's like that old saying, *"We have found the enemy, and he is us."*

You might wonder, *'What will going all out for God really cost?"* It will end up costing you everything; everything that in the final analysis doesn't really matter that much at all.

Jim Elliot, one of the five evangelists killed in 1958 by the Ecuadorian Auca tribe (Quichua word for "savage") is credited with the quote, *"He is no fool who gives what he cannot keep, to gain that which he cannot lose."*

The title of the Christian movie *"Facing the Giants,"* when coupled with the U.S. Coast Guard motto *"So that Others Might Live,"* creates a timely spiritual challenge. When combined, they put the essence of real Christian discipleship clearly before us. *"Facing the Giants"* in your life is the cost *and* the responsibility of true discipleship. *"So that Others Might Live"* is the reason why.

Are you willing to start *"Facing the Giants"* in your own life; all the hurts, fears and distractions that have held you back from going-all-out for Christ, *"So that Others Might Live?"* If we are going to achieve the spiritual breakthrough that God has for us, we must confront these hindrances as well as our own selfish nature.

As soon as possible, a one-on-one meeting with God is highly recommended. *"Today is the day of salvation."* Today is also the best time to initiate your spiritual breakthrough with God. God Almighty, the Creator of all that exists, awaits your response to His calling on your life.

Your adversary the devil, is a master of debate and stalling. He knows that if he can get you to delay getting things right with God, maybe you will never get around to it. Quite easily, the feelings and thoughts you may be experiencing today will become a faded memory. **That is why it is vitally important that you act now.**

A quick look at any of today's news broadcasts and all the unexpected and unplanned deaths ought to get your attention. Again, tomorrow is not promised. *Today is the day of salvation. Today is also the best day to become a Disciple of Truth and to take action to achieve your breakthrough.*

The devil doesn't care if you go to a revival meeting, just so long as you don't more fully commit to the plan and purposes of God. The devil doesn't particularly care if you attend church, just so long as you don't act on what you hear at the service. **The devil doesn't care if you read this book, just so long as you don't act on what you read in it.** *"Just put things off for the moment, you can always get this worked out later,"* the devil whispers. To our self-centered nature that whisper of delay makes perfect sense.

In this season of global turmoil with the growing chaos welling up all around us, it is easy to be distracted away from our God-ordained purpose. The Middle East is exploding and radical Islam is on the attack world-wide. Faith in government and political leaders is near non-existent. Upheavals in nature including hurricanes, tornadoes, wild fires and earthquakes are increasing worldwide. The world economy teeters on the brink of collapse and most people are just struggling to survive.

Granted, there are a lot of distractions to our God-ordained mission to reach the lost. How should we react to the multi-faceted demands on our attention?

The title of this chapter, "The Last Chapter" has special meaning. It applies to all of us as we look at the remainder of our lives on earth. We are powerless to change the wrongs we have committed, or somehow go back in time and make better choices. There is however, something spiritually significant that we can do. We can all **finish spiritually strong.** We can commit to the purposes of God and use whatever resources and influence we have to make a difference in the time we do have left.

God has an intended plan for everyone. Some, maybe even a few of those reading this book, have a calling on their life to be a pastor and preach the gospel. Still others may have a gift of healing that God has placed within them, that for whatever reason they have been reluctant to boldly pursue.

You might be starting to realize that all delays in fully embracing God's call on your life to reach others, has eternal consequences for all those within your sphere of influence.

All believers are called to reach family members, neighbors and friends with the gospel. Some are called to teach, others to prophesy, others to go into the domestic or foreign mission field or use a God-given musical talent in the ministry. Regardless of the many reasons that tend to hold people back from God's plan for their lives, God's gifts and calling never cease.

"For God's gifts and his call can never be withdrawn." Romans 11:29 (NLT)

There are some profound and revealing questions that can be derived from the Word of God. *"But without faith it is impossible to please Him, for he who comes to God must believe that He is, and that He is a rewarder of those who **diligently** seek Him.* Heb. 11:6 (NKJV)

This scripture challenges all Christians to honestly ask themselves, *"How am I doing when it comes to **diligently seeking Him**?"*

Another self-revealing question comes from this scripture, *"The fruit of the righteous is a tree of life; **and he that wins souls is wise.**"* Prov. 11:30 (NKJV)

The inherent question that should come to mind from this scripture is, *"How have I been doing and what am I willing to do, when it comes to the salvation of others?"*

When you finish this book or even before you finish reading it, consider responding to the stirring that you may feel within your inner being. Resolve within yourself to not let another day go by without **getting alone with God to sort out your relationship with Him**. The following might help you to initiate that "get alone with God" meeting.

Years ago I heard a preacher tell a story that to this day helps me get moving, to get doing, to somehow move me to impact the lives of those around me for the cause of Christ, even though "my flesh" lacks interest in doing so.

The story is about a father who taught his son to play chess. They were excited to hear that a chess grand master was going to visit their city. He would play all challengers simultaneously in an exhibition match open to the public.

When the day of the exhibition came, the father and son took their seats along with the many other players seated at the tables arranged so that the grand master could play from inside the many circled tables. When the games began, the grand master would come up to each table, quickly make his move and move on to the next table. In just a few minutes, after having been to all the other tables, he would again be back at their table and quickly make his next move.

Before too long, all the games were completed and the grand master had as expected, won every game. After this good time together, the father and son stopped at a restaurant to talk about the event. The son spoke of the pressure he felt during the game as the grand master moved quickly from game to game, and was back at his table before the son figured out his next move. The son said, *"The grand master was back at my table so fast it felt like it was always my move."*

There is an interesting correlation in this story, to our relationship with God. He is not waiting in heaven trying to figure out what He is going to do next in your life, in response to what you do. He knows all things, past, present and future. He knew you would be reading the words on these pages.

Jesus "made his move" and completed His task. He was obedient even to His death on the cross. He then revealed what you need to know to fulfill His plan for your life, through the Holy Spirit and His Word, the Bible.

Through the centuries, Jesus' disciples and all of His followers have carried the gospel message so people even today might believe. He knows you can't be the effective disciple He intends, without you embracing, partnering and yielding to the leading of His Holy Spirit.

Right now, the Holy Spirit of the living God stands ready as he knocks at the door of your heart and beckons you, *"Let's do this thing."* The question is, "What are you going to do?"

It's your move.

KEY STEPS TO A CHRISTIAN WALK

1. Tell others about your decision to follow Jesus Christ and to make Him the Lord of your life. Get "water baptized" as soon as you can.

2. Be prepared for the visit of the enemy (the devil) who will try to whisper in your thoughts that you are not really "saved." He'll suggest that you still have some of the old sinful desires and interests you used to have. He'll whisper that you are not like other Christians. Don't believe his lies!

   Remember, you are still a physical creature who is influenced by your soul; your mind, your will, and your emotions. As your spirit man develops, you'll begin to mature in a process called "sanctification."

   Don't believe the devil who wants to steal away and undermine God's plan for your life. Instead, believe and put your faith in Jesus, the one who proved His love for you 2,000 years ago when he paid for your sin and rebellion with His own life and shed blood.

3. Make the daily reading of God's Word and spending time with God in prayer a

priority. For many believers this is not easily accomplished because the physical nature (often referred to as the flesh) does not want to understand, yield to or prioritize the importance of serving or seeking God. It wants to stay in control.

Listen to the voice of Holy Spirit and force yourself to pursue God. As your spiritual nature strengthens, pursuing God through His Word and in prayer will become a growing source of joy, peace and fulfillment in your life.

4. Immediately begin to spend time with committed Christians who will encourage you in your pursuit of God. Enlist the aid of a mature Christian who will guide you in selecting a Bible that fits your needs.

5. Get involved with a Bible–believing church that is led by Holy Spirit of God. Find one that teaches the whole Bible and stresses the absolute importance of making Jesus the number one influence in your life.

6. Immediately stop or limit as much as possible the time spent with non-believers who will interfere or hinder your pursuit of God, (and you know who they are).

Eliminate or at least limit as much as possible the constant anti-God influence found in TV, radio, books, internet and motion pictures. Instead, listen to Christian radio, read some of the many good books and magazines available and watch great Christian internet and TV programing. These will be of great benefit and encouragement to your spiritual maturing.

If you intend to follow God's plan for your life, you must minimize your association with worldly influences. Develop friendships with true believers who will encourage you in your Christian walk.

7. Honestly identify the enemy strongholds in your life and initiate a plan to deal with them. They are stealing away your Christian effectiveness and hurting those around you. Seek out a mature Christian believer or pastor to help you in this area.

As a professing Christian, everyone around you is watching and noticing what you say and do. Begin living your life in such a manner that others may see the love of Jesus Christ reflected in you. They may then understand more about what it means to be a Disciple of Truth.

"So now I am giving you a new commandment: love each other. Just as I have loved you, you should love each other. Your love for one another will prove to the world that you are my disciples." John 13:34-35 (NLT)

"Disciples of Christ are quick to repent and quick to forgive."

Many mature Christians develop and rely on the practice of **journaling** or keeping daily notes about their Bible reading and prayer time with God. A rough, though not necessarily absolute list of the components of the practice of journaling has been condensed to:

> **Read it,**
>   **Study it,**
>   **Confess it,**
>   **Question it,**
>   **Declare it,**
>   **Celebrate it!**

Determine who, is the more spiritually mature mentor that God has placed in your life (pastor, prayer partner, life group leader, youth pastor, etc.) as well as those individuals God has placed in your life that you need to be mentoring. Begin immediately to pray about and nurture these God-ordained relationships, in order to help you in your Christian walk and also others in their spiritual maturing.

Become intimately familiar with Bible scriptures and the key components of the "Hand of Favor", "Sinners Prayer of Acceptance" and "Healing" prayers. Be ready to share these with others during the divine appointments God creates in your life. An example of the "sinners" prayer is as follows.

Dear God in Heaven - - - I come to you in the name of your son, Jesus - - - I admit I have sinned as all have sinned - - - I ask for Your forgiveness - - - I believe Jesus Christ shed His blood for my sins - - - and gave His life in order that I might have eternal life - - - I believe Jesus was raised from the dead by the power of Your Holy Spirit - - - Right now I accept Jesus as my Lord and Savior - - - With Your help, Jesus - - - I purpose in my heart - - - to serve You from this day forward. - - - In Jesus' name - - - Amen.

God's Word declares who we are; what our true identity is, in Him. Each Disciple of Truth is challenged to daily define themselves according to His Word, not the world's view point. The following page references but a few verses that confirm this.

You Are Who HE Says You Are

Psalm 45:11	You are Beautiful
Psalm 139:13	You are Unique
Jeremiah 31:3	You are Loved
Ephesians 2:10	You are Special
Jeremiah 29:11	You are Created with a Purpose
Ephesians 3: 17-19	You are Created for His Love
Daniel 12:3	You are Created to Shine
I Corinthians 6:20	You are Precious
Psalm 18: 35	You are Strong
I Peter 2:9	You are Important
Psalm 103: 12	You are Forgiven
2 Corinthians 5: 17	You are a New Creation
Psalm 121: 3	You are Protected
Philippians 4: 13	You are Empowered
John 15: 16	You are Chosen
Ephesians 2: 19	You are Family

A DISCIPLE'S CHECK LIST

1. Have you declared to others your belief in Christ and your commitment to follow Him?
2. When is your targeted one-on-one, intimate alone-time with God?
3. How is your library of memorized scriptures going, and what is your plan to expand it?
4. Have you reached that *"totally sold out to God"* moment? If not, what is your plan to dislodge what is holding you back?
5. Have you diligently sought the *"baptism in the Holy Spirit"* in order to partner with Him and open yourself to the gifts God wants to make available to you?
6. Who, and what situations, are on the "prayer list" you're starting and will remain faithful to?
7. Who is the spiritual mentor(s) that God is leading you to?
8. Who are the people that need you *to mentor and guide them* in their spiritual walk?
9. Begin using the *"God's Hand of Favor"*, *"Sinner's Prayer of Acceptance"* and the *"Prayer for Healing"* prayers, **or whatever tools** God is making you aware of, to impact others with the power of God's love?

10. Continually examine your own spiritual walk and the motives that drive your actions. If your motives are right, if your intent is to build God's Kingdom and if you have the best interest of others at heart, you are duly authorized and deputized to speak God's truth into the lives of others and demonstrate His power and love.

Actually, you are commanded to.

"And as you go, preach, saying, 'The kingdom of heaven is at hand.' Heal the sick, cleanse the lepers, raise the dead, cast out demons. Freely you have received, freely give." Mt.10: 7-8 (NKJV)

"Go therefore and make disciples of all the nations, baptizing them in the name of the Father and of the Son and of the Holy Spirit, teaching them to observe all things that I have commanded you; and lo, I am with you always, even to the end of the age. Amen." Mt. 28: 19-20 (NKJV)

THREE HEPLFUL PRAYER TEMPLETS

These suggested prayer templets can be useful tools to impact people lives, when the situation is right and the Holy Spirit is involved and leading. Remember Jesus said, ... *"for without Me, you can do nothing."* (John 15:5 NKJV)

PRAYING GOD'S HAND OF FAVOR
(prayer templet to invite God to answer a prayer)

A SINNER'S PRAYER OF ACCEPTANCE
(prayer templet for leading someone to the Lord)

A PRAYER FOR HEALING
(prayer templet to declare God's healing)

These templates and outlines are not written in stone. They can be used along with other "weapons" God brings into your spiritual arsenal.

~~~~~~~~~~~~~~~~~~~~~~~~~~~~~~~~~

GOD'S HAND OF FAVOR
(prayer templet to invite God to answer a prayer)

Most people, especially those new in their Christian walk, are reluctant to approach another with the intention of impacting their life with the presence and power of God's love. They may perceive this act as pushing their church or faith on others.

Over the years and after numerous attempts to come up with an easy non-threatening way to share God's love with others, the *"GOD'S HAND OF FAVOR"* prayer was developed. I have shared this prayer numerous times and have seen many prayers answered as a result. A brief script outline is as follows for you to use to share the *GOD'S HAND OF FAVOR* prayer with others.

It is a quick, easy and impactful approach that believers can use to touch others with God's love. This can be initiated with someone you don't even know, as well as with people you know well. Given the proper conditions and available time in a situation, **and with the prompting and presence of the Holy Spirit's leading me, I ask,**

Me, *"Do you have a quick minute?*
"Have you ever heard of the expression 'God's hand of favor?' (They may be familiar with it or if not, just add), *"It just means that God can favor whomever or do whatever He wants to do.* (I usually add something like), *"If God's favor wasn't with David when he faced the giant, things*

probably wouldn't have worked out too well."
(At this point most people smile and understand the concept.)
(Then I say), *"I want you to think for a minute. If God's hand of favor was hovering over us right now, is there somewhere in your life that you would want Him to move His hand of favor in a positive way? You do not have to tell me what it is. It may be a financial need or it could be that someone's sick or it may be about a relationship, it doesn't matter what it is. If it matters to you, it matters to God."*
(Give them a moment to think about something then ask), *"Do you have something in mind?"*
(When they nod or otherwise indicate that they do say) *"Well, let's pray right now!--- Dear God in heaven, we come to you in Jesus name, the highest way we know. Now Father, I don't know what the concern is, but you do. Right now we come together in agreement and ask that Your hand of favor would get involved in this situation in a positive way, so much so, that in days not far off he/she would know that You've heard and answered this prayer and because of this his/her faith would grow even more. Amen"*
(Then I usually say), *"Now I don' know when, maybe today, tomorrow or next week, I believe you are going to have what I call that, 'I wonder if' moment. It could be the way someone says something or a phone call received, or maybe something seen on TV that makes you wonder if*

God heard and answered this prayer. When that happens, you say the three magic words." (They may begin to look cautiously at what you are about to say, but continue and finish by telling them the three magic words, *"Thank You Lord!"* (I then add), *"God does stuff for us all the time and we're usually too busy to notice with our jobs, our phones or whatever distracts us. When we are grateful and thank Him, God is well pleased. The truth is we can live in God's hand of favor if we just remain thankful for all He has done and is doing in our lives."*

Upon praying this prayer, an immediate change in the countenance of that person often takes place. Sometimes tears well up in their eyes just because out of the blue, someone took time to pray about a concern that they have been carrying around with them. This interaction may even be an answer to their prayer where they know God sees them and understands their situation. The really great part is that when God answers the prayer of concern of their heart, you're not even around and God gets all the glory! Just stopping to pray with someone lays the groundwork for God to show Himself strong, and for that person's faith to increase as their life is touched by the power of God's love.

"Call to Me, and I will answer you, and show you great and mighty things, which you do not know." Jeremiah 33:3 (NLT)

A SINNER'S PRAYER OF ACCEPTANCE
(prayer templet for leading someone to the Lord)

The bible says in Romans 10:9-10, *"If you **confess** with your mouth that Jesus is Lord and **believe** in your heart that God raised him from the dead, you will be **saved**. For it is by **believing** in your heart that you are made right with God, and it is by **confessing** with your mouth that you are **saved**."*

Our Christian walk begins with our declaration of acknowledging and accepting Jesus' sacrifice for our sins and our intention to follow him. When people are at a point of knowing they should get things right with God, what I do is say a little prayer with them. So they don't worry about what the prayer says, I tell them ahead of time. It goes like this.

"Dear God in Heaven - - - I come to you in the name of your son, Jesus - - - I admit I have sinned as all have sinned - - - I ask for Your forgiveness - - - I believe Jesus Christ shed His blood for my sins - - - and gave His life in order that I might have eternal life - - - I believe Jesus was raised from the dead by the power of Your Holy Spirit - - - Right now, I accept Jesus as my Lord and Savior - - - With Your help, Jesus - - - I purpose in my heart - - - to serve You from this day forward. - - - In Jesus' name - - - Amen.

I ask, *"Did that sound OK?"* If they indicate they're okay with what they've just heard, continue with, *"When do you plan to pray and accept Jesus as your Savior and Lord?"* If they indicate they are ready, slowly begin to repeat the sinner's prayer you just recited. Say it the same way, not deviating or adding anything. To change the wording that they just heard and approved of will break the sincerity of the moment. If you say the first words and they follow silently mouthing the words, stop and tell them *"You don't have to shout the words, you can say them softly, just so that the breath of your words gets into the air."* Continue with the prayer, slowly giving them time to focus on what they're saying. Using a slow and deliberate cadence allows them to easily follow your lead.

Once finished with the prayer, welcome them into the family of God and use the "Key Steps to a Christian Walk" located on page 229 of this book to guide them in the next days of their Christian walk... If they are not attending a church, invite them to yours or suggest one or two full gospel churches that are located reasonably close to where they live. Let them know you are available as a resource to guide them. If appropriate, exchange information on how you can stay in contact with one another.

You can finish your time together with a prayer of protection on what God has begun in their lives, and His faithfulness to complete the good work He has started with them. (Phil. 1:6)

A PRAYER FOR HEALING
(Prayer templet to ask for God's healing)

In order to start building faith in someone who needs healing, share healing scriptures and stories of healings. If there are unbelieving people present, as best as you are able, distance them from the area where you are planning to pray for healing. You don't want their unbelief to compromise the faith and belief you are encouraging.

Let them know God wants to heal them, Jesus paid the price and our part is just to believe.

† Let them know God is able and wants to heal them.

"Beloved, **I pray that you may prosper in all things and be in health***, just as your soul prospers."* 3 John 1:2 (NKJV)

† Let them know Jesus has done His part and already paid the price and suffered for their healing.

"But He was wounded for our transgressions, He was bruised for our iniquities; The chastisement for our peace was upon Him, **And by His stripes we are healed***."* Isaiah 53:5(NKJV)

"He sent His word and healed them, And delivered them from their destructions."

Psalms 107:20 (NKJV)

*"Who Himself bore our sins in His own body on the tree, that we, having died to sins, might live for righteousness--**by whose stripes you were healed**."* 1 Peter 2:24 (NKJV)

"Most assuredly, I say to you, he who believes in Me, the works that I do he will do also; and greater works than these he will do, because I go to My Father. **And whatever you ask in My name, that I will do, that the Father may be glorified in the Son. If you ask anything in My name, I will do it."** John 14:12-14 (NKJV)

† Finish with the scripture about anointing the sick with oil; the anointing oil that you hopefully have with you.

"Is anyone among you sick? Let him call for the elders of the church, and let them pray over him, anointing him with oil in the name of the Lord. **And the prayer of faith will save the sick, and the Lord will raise him up. . . .**"
James 5:14-15 (NKJV)

Anoint them with oil in the name of the Lord as you lay hands on them. Invite the presence of the Holy Spirit as you pray along these lines:

"Dear God in heaven, we come to you in Jesus' name, the living Son of the living God. We believe that the stripes Jesus bore in His body

reach across time to heal the infirmity, the disease, and all the physical and emotional scars this person has encountered. We declare our belief in the power of Jesus' stripes, to heal every affliction and every attack of the enemy against them. We cast down every imagination of unbelief the enemy uses. We place our faith and trust and expectation of healing in the completed work of Jesus. In Jesus name, we bind every physical and spiritual attack of the enemy and we invite the Spirit of the living God to set in right order this body that was fearfully and wonderfully made by You. All these things we ask for, believe for and expect to see accomplished, in mighty name of Jesus, to the glory of God the Father, AMEN."

Upon departing, encourage the sick person and those who prayed to expect to see God answer this prayer.

"He did not waver at the promise of God through unbelief, but was strengthened in faith, giving glory to God, and being fully convinced that what He had promised He was also able to perform." Romans 4:20-21 (NKJV)

SAMPLE OF HELPFUL SCRIPTURES
(Highlight the ones that stand out and review them often.)

Then Jesus said to those Jews who believed Him, "If you abide in My word, you are My disciples indeed. And you shall know the truth, and the truth shall make you free." John 8:31-32 (NKJV)

"By this all will know that you are My disciples, if you have love for one another." John 13:35 (NKJV)

For God so loved the world that He gave His only begotten Son, that whoever believes in Him should not perish but have everlasting life. For God did not send His Son into the world to condemn the world, but that the world through Him might be saved. John 3:16-17 (NKJV)

Heaven and earth will pass away, but My words will by no means pass away. Mt. 24:35 (NKJV)

But He answered and said, "It is written, Man shall not live by bread alone, but by every word that proceeds from the mouth of God."
Mt. 4:4 (NKJV)

If you openly declare that Jesus is Lord and believe in your heart that God raised him from the dead, you will be saved. For it is by believing in your heart that you are made right with God, and it is by openly declaring your faith that you are saved. **Romans 10:9-10 (NLT)**

If My people who are called by My name will humble themselves, and pray and seek My face, and turn from their wicked ways, then I will hear from heaven, and will forgive their sin and heal their land. **2 Chron. 7:14 (NKJV)**

The Lord is my shepherd; I shall not want. He makes me to lie down in green pastures; He leads me beside the still waters. He restores my soul; He leads me in the paths of righteousness For His name's sake. Yea, though I walk through the valley of the shadow of death, I will fear no evil; For You are with me; Your rod and Your staff, they comfort me You prepare a table before me in the presence of my enemies; You anoint my head with oil; My cup runs over. Surely goodness and mercy shall follow me All the days of my life; And I will dwell in the house of the Lord Forever. **Psalms 23:1-6 (NKJV)**

But be doers of the word, and not hearers only, deceiving yourselves. **James 1:22 (NKJV)**

For the Lord Himself will descend from heaven with a shout, with the voice of an archangel, and with the trumpet of God. And the dead in Christ will rise first. Then we who are alive and remain shall be caught up together with them in the

clouds to meet the Lord in the air. And thus we shall always be with the Lord. Therefore comfort one another with these words.
1 Thess. 4:16-18 (NKJV)

Abstain from every form of evil. 1 Thess. 5:22 (NKJV)

These people draw near to Me with their mouth, And honor Me with their lips, But their heart is far from Me. And in vain they worship Me, Teaching as doctrines the commandments of men. Mt. 15: 8-9 (NKJV)

The thief's purpose is to steal and kill and destroy. My purpose is to give them a rich and satisfying life. John 10:10 (NLT)

Three things will last forever—faith, hope, and love—and the greatest of these is love.
1 Cor. 13:13 (NLT)

By this you know the Spirit of God: Every spirit that confesses that Jesus Christ has come in the flesh is of God, and every spirit that does not confess that Jesus Christ has come in the flesh is not of God. And this is the spirit of the Antichrist, which you have heard was coming, and is now already in the world. 1 John 4: 2-3 (NKJV)

For the flesh lusts against the Spirit, and the Spirit against the flesh; and these are contrary to one another, so that you do not do the things that you wish. Gal. 5: 17 (NKJV)

Now the works of the flesh are manifest, which are *these*; Adultery, fornication, uncleanness, lasciviousness, Idolatry, witchcraft, hatred, variance, emulations, wrath, strife, seditions, heresies, Envyings, murders, drunkenness, revellings, and such like: of the which I tell you before, as I have also told you in time past, that they which do such things shall not inherit the kingdom of God. *"But the Holy Spirit produces this kind of fruit in our lives:* **love, joy, peace, patience, kindness, goodness, faithfulness, gentleness, and self-control.** *There is no law against these things!"* Gal. 5:17-23 (NLT)

Do not be deceived, God is not mocked; for whatever a man sows, that he will also reap. For he who sows to his flesh will of the flesh reap corruption, but he who sows to the Spirit will of the Spirit reap everlasting life. Gal. 6:7-8 (NKJV)

And let us not grow weary while doing good, for in due season we shall reap if we do not lose heart. Gal. 6: 9 (NKJV)

Assuredly, I say to you, whatever you bind on earth will be bound in heaven, and whatever you loose on earth will be loosed in heaven. Again I say to you that if two of you agree on earth concerning anything that they ask, it will be done for them by My Father in heaven. For where two or three are gathered together in My name, I am there in the midst of them. Mt. 18:18-20 (NKJV)

Then Peter came to Him and said, "Lord, how often shall my brother sin against me, and I forgive him? Up to seven times?" Jesus said to him, "I do not say to you up to seven times, but up to seventy times seven." Mt. 18:21-22 (NKJV)

Do not lay up for yourselves treasures on earth, where moth and rust destroy and where thieves break in and steal; but lay up for yourselves treasures in heaven, where neither moth nor rust destroys and where thieves do not break in and steal. For where your treasure is, there your heart will be also. Mt. 6:19-21 (NKJV)

Ask, and it will be given to you; seek, and you will find; knock, and it will be opened to you. For everyone who asks receives, and he who seeks finds, and to him who knocks it will be opened. Mt. 7:7-8 (NKJV)

Train up a child in the way he should go, And when he is old he will not depart from it.
Prov. 22:6 (NKJV)

So then faith comes by hearing, and hearing by the word of God. **Romans 10:17 (NKJV)**

The rod and rebuke give wisdom, but a child left to himself brings shame to his mother. **Prov. 29:15 (NKJV)**

Enter by the narrow gate; for wide is the gate and broad is the way that leads to destruction, and there are many who go in by it. Because narrow is the gate and difficult is the way which leads to life, and there are few who find it. **Mt. 7:13-14 (NKJV)**

Not everyone who says to Me, 'Lord, Lord,' shall enter the kingdom of heaven, but he who does the will of My Father in heaven. Many will say to Me in that day, 'Lord, Lord, have we not prophesied in Your name, cast out demons in Your name, and done many wonders in Your name?' And then I will declare to them, 'I never knew you; depart from Me, you who practice lawlessness! **Mt. 7:21-23 (NKJV)**

Then He said to them, "The harvest truly is great, but the laborers are few; therefore pray the Lord of the harvest to send out laborers into His harvest." **Mt 9: 37-38 (NLT)**

And when He had called His twelve disciples to Him, He gave them power over unclean spirits, to cast them out, and to heal all kinds of sickness and all kinds of disease. Mt. 10:1 (NKJV)

Then they cried out to the Lord in their trouble, And He saved them out of their distresses. He sent His word and healed them, And delivered them from their destructions. Psalms 107:19-20 (NKJV)

And as you go, preach, saying, 'The kingdom of heaven is at hand.' Heal the sick, cleanse the lepers, raise the dead, cast out demons. Freely you have received, freely give. Mt. 10:7-8 (NKJV)

And you will be hated by all for My name's sake. But he who endures to the end will be saved. Mt. 10:22 (NKJV)

Therefore whoever confesses Me before men, him I will also confess before My Father who is in heaven. But whoever denies Me before men, him I will also deny before My Father who is in heaven. Mt. 10: 32-33 (NKJV)

But I say to you that for every idle word men may speak, they will give account of it in the day of judgment. For by your words you will be justified, and by your words you will be condemned. Mt. 12: 36-37 (NKJV)

Nor is there salvation in any other, for there is no other name under heaven (Jesus) given among men by which we must be saved. Acts 4:12 (NKJV)

Also a multitude gathered from the surrounding cities to Jerusalem, bringing sick people and those who were tormented by unclean spirits, and they were all healed. Acts 5:16 (NKJV)

So they said, "Believe on the Lord Jesus Christ, and you will be saved, you and your household. Acts 16: 31 (NKJV)

For I am not ashamed of the gospel of Christ, for it is the power of God to salvation for everyone who believes, for the Jew first and also for the Greek. Romans 1:16 (NKJV)

. . . For all have sinned and fall short of the glory of God. Romans 3: 23 (NKJV)

And so, dear brothers and sisters, I plead with you to give your bodies to God because of all he has done for you. Let them be a living and holy sacrifice—the kind he will find acceptable. This is truly the way to worship him. Don't copy the behavior and customs of this world, but let God transform you into a new person by changing the way you think. Then you will learn to know

God's will for you, which is good and pleasing and perfect. Romans 12:1-2 (NLT)

For the wages of sin is death, but the gift of God is eternal life in Christ Jesus our Lord. Romans 6:23 (NKJV)

But if the Spirit of Him who raised Jesus from the dead dwells in you, He who raised Christ from the dead will also give life to your mortal bodies through His Spirit who dwells in you.
Romans 8:11 (NKJV)

But God demonstrates His own love toward us, in that while we were still sinners, Christ died for us. Much more then, having now been justified by His blood, we shall be saved from wrath through Him. Romans 5: 8-9 (NKJV)

For to be carnally minded is death, but to be spiritually minded is life and peace. Because the carnal mind is enmity against God; for it is not subject to the law of God, nor indeed can be. So then, those who are in the flesh cannot please God. Romans 8: 6-8 (NKJV)

If you then, being evil, know how to give good gifts to your children, how much more will your heavenly Father give the Holy Spirit to those who ask Him." Luke 11:13 (NKJV)

For the message of the cross is foolishness to those who are perishing, but to us who are being saved it is the power of God. 1 Cor. 1:18 (NKJV)

Therefore God also gave them up to uncleanness, in the lusts of their hearts, to dishonor their bodies among themselves, who exchanged the truth of God for the lie, and worshiped and served the creature rather than the Creator, who is blessed forever. Amen. For this reason God gave them up to vile passions. For even their women exchanged the natural use for what is against nature. Likewise also the men, leaving the natural use of the woman, burned in their lust for one another, men with men committing what is shameful, and receiving in themselves the penalty of their error which was due.
Romans 1: 24-27 (NKJV)

Peter replied, "Each of you must repent of your sins and turn to God, and be baptized in the name of Jesus Christ for the forgiveness of your sins. Then you will receive the gift of the Holy Spirit. This promise is to you, to your children, and to those far away - all who have been called by the Lord our God." Acts 2: 38-39 (NLT)

And we know that all things work together for good to those who love God, to those who are the called according to His purpose.
Romans 8: 28 (NKJV)

"For I know the plans I have for you, says the Lord. They are plans for good and not for disaster, to give you a future and a hope. In those days when you pray, I will listen. If you look for me wholeheartedly, you will find me." Jer. 29:11-13 (NLT)

The fear of the Lord is the beginning of knowledge, But fools despise wisdom and instruction. Prov. 1: 7 (NKJV)

Trust in the Lord with all your heart, And lean not on your own understanding; In all your ways acknowledge Him, And He shall direct your paths. Prov. 3: 5-6 (NKJV)

The thief does not come except to steal, and to kill, and to destroy. I have come that they may have life, and that they may have it more abundantly. John 10: 10 (NKJV)

Behold, I give you the authority to trample on serpents and scorpions, and over all the power of the enemy, and nothing shall by any means hurt you. Nevertheless do not rejoice in this, that the spirits are subject to you, but rather rejoice because your names are written in heaven. Luke10: 19-20 (NKJV)

Do not withhold good from those to whom it is due, when it is in the power of your hand to do so. **Prov. 3: 27 (NKJV)**

My son, give attention to my words; Incline your ear to my sayings. Do not let them depart from your eyes; Keep them in the midst of your heart; for they are life to those who find them, And health to all their flesh **Prov. 4: 20-22 (NKJV)**

These six things the Lord hates, Yes, seven are an abomination to Him: A proud look, A lying tongue, Hands that shed innocent blood, A heart that devises wicked plans, Feet that are swift in running to evil, A false witness who speaks lies, And one who sows discord among brethren. **Prov. 6: 16-19 (NKJV)**

If you ignore criticism, you will end in poverty and disgrace; if you accept criticism, you will be honored. **Prov. 13:18 (NLT)**

If you refuse to discipline your children, it proves you don't love them; if you love your children, you will be prompt to discipline them. **Prov. 13: 24 (NLT)**

There is a path before each person that seems right, but it ends in death. **Prov. 14: 12 (NLT)**

A gentle answer turns away wrath, but harsh words stir up anger. Prov. 15:1 (NLT)

Pride goes before destruction, And a haughty spirit before a fall. Prov. 16:18 (NKJV)

Beloved, I pray that you may prosper in all things and be in health, just as your soul prospers. 3 John 1: 2 (NKJV)

Death and life are in the power of the tongue, And those who love it will eat its fruit. Prov. 18: 21 (NKJV)

He who finds a wife finds a good thing, And obtains favor from the Lord. Prov. 18:22 (NKJV)

Wine is a mocker, Strong drink is a brawler, And whoever is led astray by it is not wise.
Prov. 20:1 (NKJV)

Every way of a man is right in his own eyes, But the Lord weighs the hearts. Prov. 21: 2 (NKJV)

"Yes, I am the vine; you are the branches. Those who remain in me, and I in them, will produce much fruit. For apart from me you can do nothing. Anyone who does not remain in me is thrown away like a useless branch and withers. Such branches are gathered into a pile to be burned." John 15: 5-6 (NLT)

"We tell you this directly from the Lord: We who are still living when the Lord returns will not meet him ahead of those who have died. For the Lord himself will come down from heaven with a commanding shout, with the voice of the archangel, and with the trumpet call of God. First, the Christians who have died will rise from their graves. Then, together with them, we who are still alive and remain on the earth will be caught up in the clouds to meet the Lord in the air. Then we will be with the Lord forever. So encourage each other with these words."
1 Thess. 4:18 (NLT)

Rejoice always, pray without ceasing, in everything give thanks; for this is the will of God in Christ Jesus for you. Do not quench the Spirit. Do not despise prophecies. Test all things; hold fast what is good. Abstain from every form of evil. I Thess. 5: 16-22 (NKJV)

And they have defeated him by the blood of the Lamb and by their testimony. And they did not love their lives so much that they were afraid to die. Rev 12:11 (NLT)

Another reason for right living is that you know how late it is; time is running out. Wake up, for the coming of our salvation is nearer now than when we first believed. The night is almost gone; the day of salvation will soon be here. So don't

live in darkness. Get rid of your evil deeds. Shed them like dirty clothes. Clothe yourselves with the armor of right living, as those who live in the light. We should be decent and true in everything we do, so that everyone can approve of our behavior. Don't participate in wild parties and getting drunk, or in adultery and immoral living, or in fighting and jealousy. But let the Lord Jesus Christ take control of you, and don't think of ways to indulge your evil desires.
Romans 13:11-14 (NLT)

Jesus saith unto him, "Thomas, because you have seen Me, you have believed. Blessed *are* those who have not seen and *yet* have believed. And truly Jesus did many other signs in the presence of His disciples, which are not written in this book; but these are written that you may believe that Jesus is the Christ, the Son of God, and that believing you may have life in His name.
John 20: 29-31 (NKJV)

Work at living in peace with everyone, and work at living a holy life, for those who are not holy will not see the Lord. Heb. 12: 14 (NLT)

And let us not grow weary while doing good, for in due season we shall reap if we do not lose heart. Therefore, as we have opportunity, let us do good to all, especially to those who are of the household of faith. Gal. 6: 9-10 (NKJV)

"If I could speak in any language in heaven or on earth but didn't love others, I would only be making meaningless noise like a loud gong or a clanging cymbal. If I had the gift of prophecy, and if I knew all the mysteries of the future and knew everything about everything, but didn't love others, what good would I be? And if I had the gift of faith so that I could speak to a mountain and make it move, without love I would be no good to anybody. If I gave everything I have to the poor and even sacrificed my body, I could boast about it; but if I didn't love others, I would be of no value whatsoever.   Love is patient and kind. Love is not jealous or boastful or proud or rude. Love does not demand its own way. Love is not irritable, and it keeps no record of when it has been wronged. It is never glad about injustice but rejoices whenever the truth wins out. Love never gives up, never loses faith, is always hopeful, and endures through every circumstance. Love will last forever, but prophecy and speaking in unknown languages and special knowledge will all disappear. Now we know only a little, and even the gift of prophecy reveals little! But when the end comes, these special gifts will all disappear. It's like this: When I was a child, I spoke and thought and reasoned as a child does. But when I grew up, I put away childish things. Now we see things imperfectly as in a poor mirror, but then we will see everything with perfect clarity. All that I know now is partial and incomplete, but then I will know everything completely, just as God knows me now. There are three things that will endure -- faith, hope, and love -- and the greatest of these is love. 1 Cor. 13: 1-13 (NLT)

A final word: Be strong with the Lord's mighty power. Put on all of God's armor so that you will be able to stand firm against all strategies and tricks of the Devil. For we are not fighting against people made of flesh and blood, but against the evil rulers and authorities of the unseen world, against those mighty powers of darkness who rule this world, and against wicked spirits in the heavenly realms. Use every piece of God's armor to resist the enemy in the time of evil, so that after the battle you will still be standing firm. Stand your ground, putting on the sturdy belt of truth and the body armor of God's righteousness. For shoes, put on the peace that comes from the Good News, so that you will be fully prepared. In every battle you will need faith as your shield to stop the fiery arrows aimed at you by Satan. Put on salvation as your helmet, and take the sword of the Spirit, which is the word of God. Eph. 6: 10-18 (NLT)

God has given each one of you a gift from his great variety of spiritual gifts. Use them well to serve one another. I Peter 4: 10 (NLT)

Dear brothers and sisters, when troubles of any kind come your way, consider it an opportunity for great joy. For you know that when your faith is tested, your endurance has a chance to grow. James 1: 2-3 (NLT)

Now may the God of hope fill you with all joy and peace in believing, that you may abound in hope by the power of the Holy Spirit. Romans 15:13 (NKJV)

Devote yourselves to prayer with an alert mind and a thankful heart. Col. 4: 2 (NLT)

Live wisely among those who are not believers, and make the most of every opportunity. Let your conversation be gracious and attractive so that you will have the right response for everyone. Col. 4: 5-6

The fruit of the righteous is a tree of life, *And he who wins souls is wise.* Prov. 11:30 (NKJV)

Now faith is the substance of things hoped for, the evidence of thing not seen. Heb. 11:1 (NKJV)

So Jesus answered and said to them, *"Have faith in God."* Mark 11:22 (NKJV)

The following is a brief list of Christian books that can help you grow in your spiritual walk. They represent a very small sampling of great Christian books. Continually reading these types of transforming resources can significantly enhance your spiritual maturity.

A.W. Tozer	-	The Pursuit of God
Andrew Murray	-	Humility
Andrew Murray	-	Absolute Surrender
Bill Johnson	-	Hosting the Presence
Bill Johnson	-	The Supernatural Power of a Transformed Mind
C. S. Lewis	-	Mere Christianity
Carrol Garlington	-	The Illuminator-little ships
Cesar Castellanos	-	The Revelation of the Cross
David Platt	-	Radical
Dudley Bienvenu	-	You Can't Make it Alone
E. W. Kenyon	-	Two Kinds of Righteousness
Francis Chan	-	Crazy Love
Harry R. Jackson Jr.	-	The Way of the Warrior
Mark & Patti Virkler	-	How to Hear God's Voice
Max Anders	-	30 Days to Understanding the Christian Life
Max Lacado	-	And the Angels Were Silent
Stormie Omartian	-	Lead Me, Holy Spirit
Jason Frenn	-	The Seven Prayers God Always Answers
Francis Frangipane	-	The Three Battlegrounds
Charles Stanley	-	The Gift of Forgiveness
Lester Sumrall	-	The Gifts and Ministries of the Holy Spirit
Jentezen Franklin	-	Fasting
Charles H. Kraft	-	I Give You Authority
Kenneth E. Hagin	-	Understanding the Anointing

Jesus said to him,
*"I am the way, the truth, and the life.
No one comes to the Father except through Me.*
John 14:6 (NKJV)

The Heart of True Discipleship:
"Dear God in heaven, help me to become and to be who You desire me to be, in order that I might help others become who You desire them to be."

BECOMING A DISCIPLE" OF TRUTH TOPIC LOCATOR

TOPIC	FOUND ON PAGE(S)
666	179
A MEASURE OF FAITH	211, 212
ARMOR OF GOD	161, 162, 164, 166, 260
A SINNERS PRAYER	5, 61, 62, 233, 235, 239
A TALE OF TWO NATIONS	179
A WAY OF ESCAPING TEMPTATION	87
ABORTION	66, 134, 148, 149
ADVERSITY'S SILVER LINING	61
AMBASSADORS OF GOD'S LOVE	48, 77, 78, 80, 83, 84
ANTI-CHRIST	193
ARCHANGELS	141, 143, 144, 203, 245, 257
ARMAGEDDON	209
BABY DEDICATION	118
BACKSLIDING	174, 177
BAPTISM IN THE HOLY SPIRIT	119, 120, 126, 133, 134, 233
BEHEADINGS	40
BELIVER AGREEMENT& DELIVERENCE	159
BOTTOMLESS PIT	205-206
CASTLES vs. BUILDING THE KINGDOM	66-68, 71
CALIPH	200
CALIPHATE	200
CHAUFFER STORY	175
CHILD OF FLESH	180
CHILD OF PROMISE	181
CHRISLAM	194
CHRISTIAN WEAPONS OF WAR	161
COMMUNISM	65, 196, 198, 199, 202
DECEPTION OF COMPROMISE	147, 150, 152
DELIVERENCE	59, 60
DEMONS AND FALLEN ANGELS	144, 205
EARTHQUAKES	209
ECUADORIAN AUCA TRIBE STORY	223
ENCOMPASSING COMMANDMENTS	106
ENEMY STRONGHOLDS	153, 229
ESCAPING "LUKEWARM"	87
ESCAPING TEMPTATION	87-89

FAIR WEATHER CHRISTIANS	50
FALL OF SATAN	19
FALLEN ANGELS	142, 144, 205
FASTING	111, 169, 168
FIERY DARTS	162, 163, 165
FINISHING SPIRITUALLY STRONG	223
FORGIVENESS	28, 33, 62, 134, 140, 231, 239, 253
FRUITS OF THE HOLY SPIRIT	127
GAY AND LESBIAN LIFESTYLE	67, 139, 149
GIFTS OF THE HOLY SPIRIT	126, 135, 136, 158
GOD GIVES JEWS THE LAND	182
GOD'S HAND OF FAVOR	81-84, 169, 223, 236-238
GOD'S HAND OF FAVOR PRAYER	236
GREAT FALLING AWAY	66, 69, 184, 185
GREAT WHITE HARVEST	212, 213
HEALING PRAYERS	235,
HEALING	Over 50 references
HEAVEN IS OPTIONAL	55
HOLY SPIRIT CONVICTION	125, 131
IN ONE ACCORD	117
INFANT BAPTISM	118
INTENTIONAL DELIBERATE CHRISTIAN	30-32
INTERCESSORY PRAYER	169
ISIS	186, 196
JESUS SECOND COMMING	203, 204, 205, 207, 209
JEWISH PERSECUTION	187, 191
JIHAD	49, 179, 200, 201
KNOWING GOD	46, 210
LAKE OF FIRE	19, 56, 205, 206
LAMB'S BOOK OF LIFE	56, 60
LAWN TRIMING ANALOGY	157, 158
LEAKS IN THE BOAT	163
LIVING TOGETHER TRAP	57
MARK OF THE BEAST	179
MEMORIZING SCRIPTURE	96
MILLENNIAL REIGN OF CHRIST	199
MORAL DECLINE	139
MOUNT OF OLIVES SPLIT	205

MUHAMMAD AND ISLAM	181, 200
NO GO ZONES	201
NUCLEAR IRAN	197
NUCLEAR NORTH KOREA	197
ONCE SAVED ALWAYS SAVED	171, 174
OUR SPHERE OF INFLUENCE	219, 220
PET SIN	92
PORNOGRAPHY	44, 139, 148, 155, 156
POWER OF BELIEVER AGREEMENT	159
PRAYER LIST	169
PRAYER FOR HEALING	233, 235, 241, 263
PRESIDENT KENNEDY'S CHALLENGE	78, 79
PRIDE	19, 21-27, 32-34, 36
PROPHECY	12, 22, 39, 40, 57, 64, 101, 119, 126, 129, 130, 135, 195, 209, 259
QURAN	181, 188, 191, 201
RADICAL ISLAMC TERRORISTS	153, 155, 201
RAPTURE	114, 203-205, 207
REPENTANCE	27, 28, 33, 41, 43, 44, 51-53, 54, 58-60, 62, 63, 66, 93
SEA-DOO to SEE-DO	84
SEE-DOO OPPORTUNITIES	84
SHARIA LAW	201, 202
SPEAKING IN TONGUES	108, 126, 130, 133, 259
SPIRITUAL GIFTS	135, 137, 136, 168, 179
SPIRITUAL MENTORS	5, 79, 71, 96, 158, 233
SPIRITUAL STRONGHOLDS	153, 158, 159
SPOON-FED CHRISTIANS	95
SUBSTANCE ABUSE	16, 44, 155
SUICIDE	139-140
TEN COMMANDMENTS	104, 109, 148
THE ANCIENT SERPENT	19
THE ANTICHRIST	193, 194, 198, 203, 205
THE BOTTOMLESS PIT	205, 206
THE CHAUFFER STORY	175
THE CHESS GRAND MASTER STORY	225
THE COUNTERFIET GOD	193
THE DECEPTION OF COMPROMISE	147, 150-152

THE FAMILY OF JESUS	168
THE FLAWED ATHEIST PERSPECTIVE	37
THE WATCH STORY	37, 38
THE GREAT COMMISSION	53, 119
THE GREAT DRAGON	19
THE GREAT FALLING AWAY	66, 69, 184, 185
THE GREAT TRIBULATION	193, 199, 203-205, 209, 212
THE GREAT WHITE HARVEST	209
THE HOLY SPIRIT	140 plus ref. throughout
LIST OF WHO ENCOURAGED YOU	215
THE MILLENIAL REIGN OF CHRIST	199, 205, 20
THE PERSON OF THE HOLY SPIRIT	123
THE PHONE CALL STORY	219
THE TEN COMMANDMENTS	104, 109, 148
THE UNPARDONABLE SIN	128, 129
THE WHOLE ARMOR OF GOD	162, 164
THE WINDING ROAD OF LIFE	175, 177
THINK YOU MIGHT BE A CHRISTIAN?	43
TITHING	153, 154, 160
TRINITY DISCIPLESHIP	65, 68-70
TWO ENCOMPASING COMMANDMENS	106
UNDERSTANDING ISLAM	35, 40, 65, 179, 184, 188-190
UNDERSTANDING ISLAM cont.	191, 193, 194, 196-202, 222
UNFORGIVENESS	153-155, 168
USING A PRAYER LIST	169, 223
WATCH STORY	37
WATER BAPTISM	111, 115, 118
WOLF STORY	15-17
YESHUA vs. JESUS	35, 103
YOUR SPHERE OF INFLUENCE	13, 219, 223
YOUR STORY / HIS GLORY	73

Hopefully, this book will play at least some small part in encouraging the lost to come to a saving and intimate relationship with God through Jesus Christ, and will challenge current believers to more fully commit to God's call on their lives.

DISCIPLE'S CALLING
(All believers are called to be Disciples)

"Let your light so shine before men, that they may see your good works and glorify your Father in heaven."
Matt. 5:16

"So the disciples went and did as Jesus commanded them."
Matt. 21:6

"For whoever does the will of God is My brother and My sister and mother."
Mark 3:35

"Most assuredly, I say to you, he who believes in Me, the works that I do he will do also; and greater works than these he will do, because I go to My Father. And whatever you ask in My name, that I will do, that the Father may be glorified in the Son. If you ask anything in My name, I will do it. "If you love Me, keep My commandments. And I will pray the Father, and He will give you another Helper, that He may abide with you forever-- the Spirit of truth, whom the world cannot receive, because it neither sees Him nor knows Him; but you know Him, for He dwells with you and will be in you."
John 14:12-17

"The night is far spent, the day is at hand. Therefore let us cast off the works of darkness, and let us put on the armor of light."
Romans 13:12 (NKJV)

Copies of <u>Becoming a Disciple of Truth</u> are available online at amazon.com, directly from Brushfire Publications, and soon to be available at other Christian resource outlets.

For those who want a more detailed and comprehensive commentary on the Bible, **Halley's Bible Handbook** by Henry H. Halley is a great resource and can be found online and at bookstores worldwide.

Please direct questions, comments or statements of endorsement to: mcmilesjr@yahoo.com or call 337-781-3280

Made in the USA
Columbia, SC
27 July 2021